THE POWER OF GOD... YESTERDAY

by CHRISTINE M. BLAKE

THE POWER OF GOD...YESTERDAY

BY CHRISTINE M. BLAKE.ORG

November 2023

PUBLISHED BY THE BLESSED REASON TRIP
BLESSEDREASONTRIP@GMAIL.COM

ISBN (paperback)-13: 978-1-959926-03-0

PRINTED IN THE UNITED STATES OF AMERICA

Medical Disclaimer: This book is not intended as a substitute for the medical advice of physicians. The reader should regularly consult a physician in matters relating to his/her health and particularly with respect to any symptoms that may require diagnosis or medical attention.

Thank you to the all the holy angels and saints

who intercede daily on our behalf…

To the Holy Trinity-

God, the Father, who provided the instruction,

Jesus, who lovingly stayed beside me as I wrote,

and the Holy Spirit who gave breath to this book…

and to every miracle I have ever witnessed.

contents.

preface.

Over the past four years, I have witnessed numerous miracles. The impossible made possible, disease and sickness disappearing, all the while, many of these same individuals are further transformed into living their all for Jesus.

This book is intended to reveal where we are today and where we are going tomorrow, all derives from God's power in our lives *Yesterday*. His words from days of old are what give us the hope and courage to get through our present days and keep us looking forward with confidence. These powerful words are instrumental in helping us understand how to live, who Jesus is, how to ask, seek, knock, and have the "Blessed Hope" for what is yet to come.

I was first introduced to this amazing new way of living in 2011 when I attended a healing service with Dr. Issam Nemeh. I had never been to a healing service, had someone pray over me, or seen anything remotely like it before. On that day, I witnessed individuals of all kinds seeking healing for themselves or their loved ones. I was one of those individuals. I recall sitting there, feeling quite desperate, observing others during their prayers while I waited, wondering what would happen during our own.

My husband and I went there with the hope of finding a miracle for our youngest child, Emily. When we went to the healing service in 2011, Emily received the miracle we were looking for and was healed from a tumor on her ribs. Little did we know at the time that Emily and I would once again meet Dr. Nemeh in the future and hear those same beautiful prayers eight years later.

Amazingly, when we encountered Dr. Nemeh another time in January of 2019, Emily was healed yet again, but this time from something entirely different. This transformation occurred when I went to Dr. Nemeh's medical office for my own health concerns. Emily came along with me solely out of love and support as I traveled all the way from Iowa to Ohio for the medical appointment that I had arranged with him. I scheduled this appointment because Emily wanted me to search for alternative medicine and refused to accept the diagnosis I was given.

I have written two books about the impact that appointment made on my life. The books explain how the systemic lupus and other autoimmune issues I experienced at that time disappeared without a trace. If it were not for that most divine appointment, I would still be sick and not be spiritually living as I am now.

Remarkably, Emily's suggestion to visit him out of her love for me is what resulted in her finding healing for herself a second time. She was given another miracle from a medical issue that she had been dealing with for quite a while. It was a case of endometriosis that was both painful and severe. Since then, we have been on a fast-paced track to learn more about this Jesus who showed up in that Westlake, Ohio office during our time there.

It wasn't long before we told as many people as possible about the miracles we stumbled upon and what we thought was attainable for everyone. As a result, this change in our lives inspired many others to seek out Dr. Nemeh for their own healing prayers. We witnessed countless miracles as we followed the Holy Spirit's direction. The miracles varied, from what may have seemed small or trivial to the most incredible, lifesaving restorations being made for many.

I have learned a lot about walking with Jesus and allowing the Holy Spirit to work through me in the past four years. Without Dr. Issam Nemeh, I would not be where I am today. Without his 'yes', his fiat and surrender to our Lord for his life, none of these miracles I write about would have been possible.

I have seen and been around Dr. Nemeh enough to understand how incredible his faith is. His wisdom, gentleness, humility, and closeness to our Lord are unlike anything I have witnessed in anyone else. The miraculous happening around him is unending, and because of this, I need to take a closer look at what he says.

Jesus is quoted as saying to the Jews in John 10:29,

> *"..if I do His work, then believe in the evidence of the miraculous works I have done, even if you don't believe Me.*
>
> *Then you will know and understand that the Father is in Me, and I am in the Father."*

as well as the following later in John 14:12

> *Very truly I tell you, whoever believes in Me will do the works I have been doing, and they will do even greater things than these, because I am going to the Father.*

Regarding the works that I have observed transpiring around Dr. Nemeh, and the miracles surrounding him, I most certainly do believe in all of them. For I am one of those works!

Through Dr. Nemeh's prayers of faith, Jesus healed me. Therefore, I must also properly explore the things I have heard him speak about numerous times. Recently, I have felt called to share some specific insights that I have learned from hearing Dr. Nemeh speak, specifically about the confusing days we are currently in. This world that we live in can take a toll on a person. It seems as if society is moving away from God on almost every level. It's crucial to shift our perspective from this negative world and focus on what God is doing instead. That is what I hope this book will do for everyone who reads it. God wants us to pay attention and is trying to wake up those who aren't.

He wakes us up by showing us His love, His mercy… His miracles. The signs of His nearness are everywhere.

My daughter Emily and I have been paying close attention for almost four years now. Despite the world continuing to spin out of control at alarming rates, the "true" Christians have been demonstrating the opposite effect.

They are becoming more unified and focused, and a growing number of individuals who have not seen clearly before are now awakening. Over the past few years, Christian healing services have been popping up all over the place in both neighboring towns and parishes near and far. The stories of God's healing power are literally exploding everywhere around us. It doesn't take much to see how God is moving with unprecedented speeds, and for good reason.

John 1:1-5

In the beginning was the Word, and the Word was with God, and the Word was God. He was with God in the beginning. Through Him all things were made; without him nothing was made that has been made. In him was life, and that life was the light of all mankind. The light shines in the darkness, and the darkness has not overcome it.

one.

NOW I SEE

I recall the thoughts I had when I woke up the next day after returning home from my time with Dr. Issam Nemeh in 2019. I was able to see a whole new world around me that I wasn't ever able to perceive before. I had basically been given a spiritual wake-up call.

I have previously written about what happened to me during my office visit with Dr. Nemeh in *The Power of God... Today.* I gave a description of how Dr. Nemeh treated me in his office. During his procedure, he quietly requested the Holy Spirit to come to me and assist in removing my pain and disease. The prayers he prayed for me were quite powerful. The Holy Spirit did come, restoring a sense of joy in my heart while also removing many wounds in my body, soul, and spirit.

Dr. Nemeh assured me that I would be fine when I left that appointment. He wasn't offering false hope but rather revealing to me what had been revealed to him...if I were to walk in faith. Our faith is crucial in these matters, and we must put it into action with our belief.

Due to everything that transpired during my appointment, I was able to heal from a serious disease and other disorders. My physical healing began on a small scale and eventually increased until I was fully healed. At the same time, I was undergoing a major spiritual transformation. God was healing me on all levels. All of which testifies to the power of one man's faith that with God, anything is possible.

I was prompted to reflect on my life before that moment and the frightening place I was headed if God hadn't intervened. The truth is Jesus knew that I was truly lost. Mercifully, thanks to my daughter Emily's persistence in searching for a miracle for a disease that was ravaging my body, Jesus came and found me.

I was caught off guard that day when suddenly the Jesus I thought I knew and was "sort of" following appeared. He let me know that He is always with me, that He loves me, and that He has forgiven my many sins. I saw Him. I felt His love for me. After that day, I experienced the presence of the Holy Spirit within me, forming me day by day. I developed a strong desire to be in His daily presence forever after that. I began to incorporate prayer, worship, and spiritual disciplines to strengthen my connection with Him.

It was amazing what happened to me physically and spiritually. God healed me from systemic lupus, fibromyalgia, and several other disorders. But most importantly, I had received the greatest treasure one can ever be given from God – the gift of true faith. The intense conversion taking place inside my soul surprised me and everyone around me.

It was evident that something radical had happened during my appointment with Dr. Nemeh. My rheumatologist retested all the lab studies to confirm that my suspicions were true - I was no longer sick. My spiritual life was also flourishing, filled with activities to serve God and others. Everything that was happening to me reflected the reality of the Bible verse in John 14:6, in which Jesus declares, *"I am the Way, the Truth, and the Life."*

The Christian way of living that I had been striving for but didn't really comprehend prior had become more real than I had ever imagined. Suddenly, all the doubts I had ever had regarding the true presence of Jesus and Heaven were completely gone. On that special day, Jesus entered my life and removed a dark, thick veil from my eyes, giving me the clearest vision of my entire life. I was then set ablaze with an intense love for God that I had never felt before. Nothing has been the same for me since.

I began the search of a lifetime after that miraculous moment when Jesus pulled me in, and I felt His closeness on a level far beyond human comprehension. I was eager to discover everything I could about God, the apostles, saints, and our faith. I couldn't learn fast enough. I had a hunger that I hadn't experienced before. I continued my quest for knowledge of Him with my daughter Emily, who was likewise feeling the same pull.

We discovered a lot together. We didn't understand what we were lacking until we started the search of our lives. The Bible, the Holy Spirit, the saints, and the power of prayer helped open our eyes to some hidden truths. The fact that we could ask the Holy Spirit for help because the Spirit was actually God in action was a game-changer for us.

We both pondered, *Why had we never heard any of this before? Or at least not in the way we now could?*

We wanted everyone to know about this incredible gift that is freely available to all.

The Work of the Spirit, the Third Person of the Trinity, was first brought to life for us by Dr. Nemeh. We would hear him softly calling out to the Holy Spirit in Jesus' name when he prayed over us. With great faith, he waited for the Holy Spirit to come and never doubted.

Soon after, Emily and I began to learn how the Holy Spirit worked by being our Advocate, Teacher, Counselor, and

Communicator. It was not long before we discovered the faith to call upon and regularly walk with the Holy Spirit in our lives. At first, the reality of this spiritual side of life was challenging, but at the same time, it almost seemed too good to be true. In my heart, I kept questioning, *Why didn't we know more about these things before?*

Before my encounter with Christ and observing Dr. Nemeh's influential examples, I had never considered what being a true follower of Christ meant. Prior to that pivotal moment with Jesus, I was known as being lukewarm, as written in Revelation. I was searching for Him, but before that day, my spiritual life was mostly unremarkable. I had no idea just how lost I was until I was found.

Never in a million years would I have guessed that someone as ordinary and broken as me would be sought out by God in such a beautiful way. During that moment, I was keenly aware of my own unworthiness. I make a daily effort to never be separated from Him again. Therefore, I currently live with an eagerness to serve Christ, to wait for His promptings, and to hear His voice.

Since 2019, I have shifted from being centered on myself and my life to focusing my thoughts and heart onto God and how I could serve Him. My daughter Emily and I have worked together to educate others about the closeness of Jesus, the power of prayer, and the miracles that happen around us all every day.

As I stepped into this new role in my life, I began to understand that Jesus healed us not only for our own good but also for the sake of others. It was a gift that was meant to be shared. We told our story about this man's remarkable faith and the widespread healings that have surrounded him nearly his entire life with everyone we could. Emily and I were able to contribute to the bigger purpose that God had planned from the beginning by leading hundreds of others to Dr. Nemeh for their own prayers.

John 14:26

But the Advocate, the Holy Spirit, whom the Father will send in my name, will teach you all things and will remind you of everything I have said to you.

two.

RIPPLE EFFECT

Over the past four years, I have dedicated myself to keeping my focus on Jesus and what's possible for others through prayer. However, even with the best of intentions, there have been times when I have fallen into an unhealthy season of life. Most of the time, I didn't realize it was happening because it occurred so subtly.

This was not something I wanted or intended to do. Typically, it was due something going on in my life that required my full attention. Regrettably, this would ultimately lead me away from what I was meant to be doing and what was truly important in life. Without realizing it, I would quickly return to my lazy habits of not being spiritually minded.

My focus was intended to be on Christ and spiritual matters. But suddenly, I would go from having daily prayer routines, reading Scripture, and just being with the Lord to having days and weeks going by with nothing of the sort. I was blindly ignoring my promises to God until one day, I found myself in a pretty bad place.

In December 2022, Emily and I had just returned from a trip to see Dr. Nemeh. I was preparing to convert my second book, *The Power of God... Tomorrow*, into an audio format. I was aware that I needed to do this, but at the same time, I was in a gloomy state. I had allowed the world and all its ways to slowly but surely start trickling back into my life.

It all began in a relatively minor way. As a result of one thing leading to another, I was clogging up my life with unimportant things, leaving little time for God. The spotlight was once again on me and my life. I was not focusing on the tasks God had asked me to accomplish, such as the audiobook. I kept putting it off. I also had the adversary telling me there wasn't much else for me to achieve concerning helping people find God's healing power. The devil deceived me into believing that I had reached the end of the line and that God was done with me.

I became convinced of what I was being told. Almost immediately, I became depressed and lacked the energy to do much of anything. I should have been praying harder than ever, but I wasn't. From one day to the next, I had unintentionally allowed myself to be led astray and far away from the Lord. I was becoming spiritually lazy and inactive.

Before long, I noticed that not only did I lack energy and feel sad, but also other problems were starting to emerge. I encountered persistent knots in my neck and back on a regular basis. Lots of them. It reminded me of when I had fibromyalgia before being healed in 2019.

The new knots were just as painful as before, often, they would even burn. I was confronted with more knots, and then there was a heaviness that started developing inside my chest. This uncomfortable sensation was something I remembered all too well. It was the same, identical discomfort I used to encounter when I had the accumulation of fluid around my heart before God healed me and took it all away. I was once again struggling to breathe any time I slightly exerted myself. Even walking our dog challenged me.

Things deteriorated on a daily basis. I observed that the knots in my neck and back were also beginning to spread to my arms. It reached such an extreme level that it was even becoming worse than how I felt before my healing. I never let anyone around me know how terrible things had become. Due to the pain and the uncertainty of my situation, I often silently cried myself to sleep at night.

I was rapidly going downhill. I was desperate and started secretly scheduling massages with the hope that they would be able to alleviate the discomfort and remove the knots. Every time I went, I was scheduled with a different massage therapist. Every single one of them would express concern with how inflamed I was. Inflammation was present throughout my entire body, not just in my neck and back. They would offer their advice, such as eliminating bread and pasta from my diet or suggesting an herbal supplement that they thought might be helpful. One day, one of them recommended that I seek treatment from a chiropractor.

Upon doing so, the chiropractor made the same remarks about my inflammation. He asked me what I had been doing or taking to cause all of this trouble. I had no answers. I, myself, was unsure of what was happening.

The relief I found from the massages and the chiropractor was extremely short-lived. I would feel a bit better until I went to sleep only to wake up the next day with the pain starting all over again. I felt hopeless because I could not find a solution. I went through our medicine cabinet looking for the old muscle relaxers that were prescribed to help me sleep when I had this problem years ago. Even though I no longer needed them at that point, I kept them just in case anything came up. I never expected it to be for this reason.

I was experiencing an all-time low. Until one day, I received a phone call from another author whom I had never met in person but who I consider a cherished friend. She reached out after I had just finished having a bad crying spell. I was feeling hopeless and having a terrible day. She recounted that she was driving to pick up her mother from a doctor's visit, when there was a prompting for her to call me right away. She inquired about my day and informed me that she knew the importance of calling me immediately when the feeling arose. She stated that she never questions those moments, instead she just follows through and acts on them.

The two of us were brought together over the processes involved in making an audiobook, as well as our mutual love for the Nemehs. My dear friend informed me of how things were coming together for her to begin narrating and recording her own audiobook. I was happy to hear her strides, although it was a painful reminder for me that I hadn't followed through on my end with what I knew God was asking of me.

She thanked me for sharing what I knew about this topic the last time we spoke. I conveyed to her that she was too kind as I really didn't know much. Meanwhile, I had tears in my eyes and fought the lump in my throat as I spoke. I knew that she could sense my sadness, and it wasn't a sentence or two more when she started speaking to me about my worth. She reminded me of the people I have helped in the past.

By then, I was weeping and explained that I was feeling quite discouraged. I was experiencing a deep sadness in my spirit as I came to the realization that I had not been following through with things for God. It wasn't just that. I was also feeling quite miserable in my body. I expressed my regret for complaining about such trivial matters to her. She swiftly dismissed those comments, reminding me that everything is significant. "Everything makes a ripple effect, even in our bodies," she said.

Our conversation was brief, but when we ended it, I was overwhelmed by how God connects us to people in such a perfect way. He is always there for us, attempting to reach out to us, even by sending loving messages from others in our lives.

As meaningful as it was to have this friend reach out to me and know that God inspired her to do so, I was still wallowing in pain and despair. I thought I was hiding it all pretty well until one morning, Emily asked me out of the blue, "Mom, you're not getting your fibro back, are you?"

1 Corinthians 12:26 ESV

If one member suffers, all suffer together; if one member is honored, all rejoice together.

three.

YOUR PERSONAL JOURNEY WITH JESUS

Emily's question had a profound impact on me. Right then, I realized that I was not deceiving anyone. I also didn't want her to question the possibility of losing her own healing if this was happening to me.

I can't recall the answer I gave her when she asked me. But I clearly remember what happened when Emily left the house to go to work that morning. I ran upstairs to my office with a sense of urgency and started researching. I was curious if it's possible for someone to lose the healing that Jesus gave them. Since it was Jesus who healed me of all my sicknesses in that treatment room in Ohio with Dr. Nemeh.

After my appointment with him, I received medical confirmation that I was genuinely healed. It was unclear to me how I could be sick with the same issues I had before. If I had been sick with a new disease or illness, that would have been an entirely different situation. But I wasn't. Everything I was suffering from was exactly what was healed before through treatment and prayer.

After a long day of investigating online, I discovered that what Jesus gives is something that should always be there and never leave. It was theoretically possible for the same illness to reoccur, but it was extremely rare if it did. Usually, there is more at play than what meets the eye.

A website I came across addressed the Bible verse where Jesus heals a man and instructs him to stop sinning. Otherwise, he will become sicker than before. According to this site, if a person is healed but not fully following God's will for their life, they may lose their healing this way as well.

I was comforted by reading this, immediately taking note of how I had been living and acting when this all began. I searched my heart, and the Holy Spirit quickly enlightened me. The life I had been leading recently revealed that I was slowly inching away from God.

I wasn't intentionally doing anything wrong, but I certainly wasn't praying as much or following God's will in my life as I was before. I was becoming less spiritually minded, and worldly patterns were slowly making their way back into my life. Instead of doing God's work, I found myself wasting time watching a lot of television and scrolling on my phone. It wasn't necessarily that those things were bad in themselves. It was more that they had suddenly taken hold of me. My healing was for a significant purpose, and I must live accordingly.

There was no change on God's part. The opportunities to serve Him were still being held for me. I was the one who walked away and wasn't following through with my end of the bargain. The relief was that there was a simple fix to all of this, one that would restore everything, even the sadness I now carried with me. Pain and illness aside, my life without Christ at the center felt totally empty. I needed to renew my mind, heart, and life to return to what God desired for me.

That night, before going to bed. Immediately, out loud, I renounced Satan and all his evil ways. With all my heart, I claimed my healing. And most of all, I thanked Jesus for everything He had healed me from in Dr. Nemeh's office in January 2019 and for loving me.

I brushed my teeth and climbed into bed, asking myself, *How could I have gotten so lost?* I cried myself to sleep that night. This time my tears were not due to physical pain, but rather, my soul was overwhelmed with the sadness of allowing this to happen.

Something woke me up the following morning before my alarm went off, although I am not sure what. The sun hadn't even started coming up yet, I noticed as my eyes were squinting, trying to make out the time on my phone. I lay there contemplating the prayers I prayed before going to sleep the night before. I was also recalling everything I had learned. I came to the realization that I didn't know as much as I thought I did about how Jesus works in terms of healing people.

My mind was whirling with thoughts about everything until I noticed that I hadn't felt any pain yet. I lay there with perfect stillness, unconsciously holding my breath and frightened to investigate further.

Finally, I braved my fears, got out of bed, and moved around slowly. I had no pain in my body. I had nothing at all! I felt absolutely perfect. The knots, all of them, had left just like that. And likewise, all the pain and burning that usually accompanied them was also nonexistent. I couldn't believe it!

I was trying to trust that I had been healed when I cried out to God the night before. But truthfully, when I went to sleep, I didn't think that it was going to completely disappear overnight just like that. I believe I was anticipating a much slower recovery period, if any. It was a true testament to both why it occurred and that His promises are eternal.

I wrote Kathy Nemeh an email regarding what happened to me, ending it with:

> *I am just so thankful that God teaches us and reprimands us when needed.*
>
> *I remembered hearing in one of the podcasts Dr. Nemeh say that when he is not doing what God wants him to do, he becomes very physically sick...Boy, do I ever get it now! ...so do I!*
>
> *I just wanted to share this journey of learning with you. I am still learning from you guys...I feel like nearly on a daily basis.*
>
> *I love you Kathy and the Doc so much and can never thank you both for all you have done for me and my relationship with God. You both mean more to me than I can ever put into words. I know this goes for Emily, too.*
>
> *I told Emily I was going to write you about it...Emily's comment was, "Kathy will love this. She is always talking about the importance of teaching someone a lesson."*
>
> *Boy, God sure taught me one...one that hopefully I will NEVER forget.*

Kathy emailed back,

Dear Christy, Wow! That's incredible! It's all about staying in the "healing zone!" Always put yourself in the treatment room where you initially received the healing. It will keep you centered and focused on prayer. The Holy Spirit is alive and well in your body! All you have to do is keep it going! This is all about your personal journey with Jesus. Our prayers are always surrounding you! Love you.

The healing that God initially gave me was not meant to be in vain. It was meant for me to leave my old ways behind. No longer was I to be drifting aimlessly in life. God restored my health and time on this earth to glorify Him by doing good for others. I can't imagine how far I would have strayed from this premise without the blessing of becoming sick again.

By suffering the way I did, I was able to remember what He did for me and the purpose behind it. The pain I endured brought me back to the Lord with all my heart, hoping to never leave Him again.

It was unbelievable that I had been healed for nearly three years and then forgot so many lessons I had learned along the way. The irony was that during my low point, someone I loved very much had told me that they had also stopped praying the way they used to. However, they were fortunate to recognize it right away and, renew their prayer life and walk with the Lord.

When she told me this, I just made some absurd comment like, "Yeah, that happens in life sometimes."

I was oblivious to what was happening in my own prayer life at the time. It was exactly like the Bible verse, *"You see the speck in your brother's eye, but fail to see the log in your own eye." – Matthew 7:3-5*

There was no doubt that God had been calling my name for some time, gently trying to wake me up from the subtle spiritual slumber I had fallen into. Due to my lack of response, God proceeded to use a more extreme approach, shaking me awake. I am grateful that He never gave up on me.

In the same way, there were trials that I faced early on in my healing as well. I wrote about them in *The Power of God... Today.* The reason for these challenges was to test my heart and purify my life. Would I be able to sort out the truth? To rely on what God had done for me and to trust in the medical tests that validated it? Or would I be quick to assume that the setbacks meant I had lost the healing He gave me? The trials were specifically designed by God to reveal things about myself and which aspects of my spiritual life I needed to work on.

In this recent occurrence, though, it was me who caused the suffering. I had become overly occupied with earthly things, even just comfortable routines, and made them idols, placing them above my relationship with Jesus.

It's easy to get swept up in worldly things without any thought until God wakes us up and reveals what's really happening. Thankfully, when we get lost, God gives us the opportunity to choose Him again and again.

1Peter 1:6-7

In all this you greatly rejoice, though now for a little while you may have had to suffer grief in all kinds of trials. These have come so that the proven genuineness of your faith—of greater worth than gold, which perishes even though refined by fire—may result in praise, glory and honor when Jesus Christ is revealed.

four.

HIS WILL BE DONE

Reconnecting with God was as simple as saying those quick prayers and making God the center of my life again. Those basic actions were all that was required, and He was right there waiting for me. Through dreams and other signs, He revived His earlier plans for me to produce an audio version of my second book, *The Power of God…Tomorrow.*

I was fully committed to this new venture. Then, out of nowhere, I sensed God asking Emily and me to aid someone on their journey to Ohio for an appointment with Dr. Nemeh.

However, it seemed to me that we would be taking not only one person but two, even though I was still unsure of who they were. I knew that He was simply asking me to trust Him, and that it would perfectly fit into Emily's scheduled week off during her spring break in March.

It was already February, and I had no idea how far out they were scheduling patients at that time. Furthermore, I was unsure if there would be any appointments available during that specific period in March. I finally gave in to the nudges and contacted Dr. Nemeh's office to verify if it was possible. I discovered that they were completely booked until the end of April.

"The end of April? Oh gosh. Okay," I said, responding to the sad news. I was speaking with Shannon at Dr. Nemeh's office. I was certain that she could sense the disappointment that came through my voice.

Shannon inquired more about the specific timeframe that I was looking for. I let her know that I was hoping for some time during the week of March 13th through the 17th since that's when Emily's spring break was planned.

Shannon reviewed their schedule once more, attempting to make it work. Regrettably, it just was not possible. To make things worse, she mentioned that specific week was highly popular, and there was a waiting list for others who were trying to be squeezed in, just like us.

I was heartbroken. I didn't follow through with God's promptings as quickly as I should have. At this point, I had been feeling like He was asking this for nearly two weeks, and now I was paying the price for dragging my feet once more.

I was in deep thought about my never-ending inconsistencies in following the Holy Spirit properly when Shannon spoke up, "Christy, do you want me to add you to the wait list for those dates?"

I paused, praying for guidance on what to do. I piped up, "Sure!"

"Alright, Christy, just the one spot then?"

Chuckling nervously, I stated, "Well…no. Actually, I know this sounds sort of bizarre. Especially since there are no spots available and there is a waiting list to boot...But I think God is actually asking us to bring *two* people with us this time."

Given the circumstances, my highly unlikely request brought Shannon and I together in laughter.

I professed, "Well, whatever happens it will clearly show me if this is the Lord's will. If you have a long list right now and then have two spots become available, just like that…for that specific week, no less, we will certainly know that it is God's will. That would be a true sign from God."

Shannon agreed wholeheartedly. God would reveal to us what was meant to be.

Not too many days later, I was out shopping at a nearby grocery store. As I was walking through the frozen food aisle, a sudden smell of what could only be described as a large number of roses filled the air around me. It was incredibly strong.

I have had the chance to experience this peculiarity multiple times in the past. Previously, I would be standing by someone, whether I knew them or not, and it would be instantly made apparent that I was meant to share something with that individual. The usual reason was to invite someone to a particular healing service or bus trip to see Dr. Nemeh or something similar.

This time, in the grocery store, I stopped in my tracks as the gush of beautiful but distinct aroma blew by. I contemplated all the previous instances of this happening and how the Holy Spirit would normally direct me towards the person I was meant to speak with.

The only event we had in mind this time was a far-fetched trip to Ohio. The likelihood of going was slim since there were no appointments available, and I still had no idea who God wanted us to invite. I examined my surroundings, even doing a complete 360-degree circle, believing I was missing something. *Who am I supposed to be inviting, Lord?* I prayed.

There was no one around me at all. After being dumbfounded for a moment, I shook it off. I began to doubt if the incident had actually occurred. *Is it possible that I imagined that?*

I continued pushing my grocery cart down the aisle and into the next one until it happened once more. Still, no one was near me. I was very confused by what was taking place. Here I was, still walking through the frozen food section, so there was no way that an overwhelming scent of roses could be coming from anywhere nearby.

I prayed, expecting God to reveal the meaning of all of this to me. But nothing came from that prayer. I was partly questioning my sanity at this point. I finished my shopping, got in the car, and drove home. After entering the house and unloading the groceries from the car, I pulled out my phone from my pocket.

I noticed that I had received a text message from Dr. Nemeh's office. Shannon had sent it while I was experiencing the unexplained episodes in the grocery store. My phone never went off when the texts came through. This was because it was still in the do-not-disturb mode from the earlier Mass I had attended before going to the store. I had failed to remember to turn the ringer back on.

Shannon's text read that Dr. Nemeh had two spots open up, and she was curious if we were still interested. She mentioned that one was available on Thursday, March 16th, and another on Friday, March 17th.

I was in total awe! It was almost beyond belief, especially considering there was a waitlist just days earlier. I knew not to question how this could have possibly happened. I have seen miracles happening around Dr. Nemeh in every way, and I understood that this was just another one of those Heavenly occurrences. God had a plan in mind. My only requirement was to trust and have faith; everything else would work out just like it was supposed to.

From our previous events, I knew that from here on out, Emily and I were meant to be praying for the two people that God had a plan for. Neither of us knew who they were or how to find them. My only knowledge was that we needed to pray. He would instruct us on how to proceed. I couldn't doubt anything, especially given what just happened.

Hebrews 11:1

Now faith is confidence in what we hope for and assurance about what we do not see.

five.

A DIVINE (tax) APPOINTMENT

I remained closer to Christ than I had been in months. Working for Him, attending Mass, praying, and reading the Bible were all part of my daily routine. The feeling of being in that zone again was incredible, and I was determined to never let myself grow apart from Him again.

In early February of 2023, I woke up to a beautiful, bright morning and was searching for God's plan for the day ahead. I took advantage of the rare opportunity to experience such warmth outside early in the year and went on a quick walk with my dog. I recall not only the remarkably nice temperatures outside but also the rare sighting of two white-winged doves. For a brief moment, they flew back and forth around me. It definitely caught my attention and made me question if there was a deeper meaning behind it. Regardless of its significance, I was thankful for the experience, mainly because it brought to mind the Holy Spirit's presence, which is often portrayed to be like a dove.

Shortly thereafter, I was hurrying to get ready, gather my belongings, and drive thirty-five minutes to our annual tax appointment. Randy and I had completed our portion of the workload. The purpose of the appointment was mainly for me to give over our receipts and numbers for the year to our accountant. Our tax return would then be prepared later and filed by her using this information.

Typically, our appointments are about an hour in length, but this year, I arranged for it to be a bit longer than our usual allotted time. My intention was to discuss *The Blessed Reason Trip* organization that Emily and I established in 2019 and the possible tax benefits that would come from making it a nonprofit. It was one more thing I felt God might be calling me to do, but I was unsure how to proceed.

Anne has been our tax professional for nearly twenty years. She is a warm-hearted, sweet person whom I developed a friendly rapport with through our years together. Often, during our annual appointments, we would end up discussing matters of faith. This became especially true when she learned that I had begun writing books about the miracles that God had accomplished in the lives of many people around us.

I was anticipating seeing her, but upon entering her office, I sensed something was not right. She didn't look like herself. Her eyes were puffy and red. At first glance, I thought she might be fighting a cold or allergies. However, it wasn't long before I began to believe that it was much more serious than that.

I was clinging to God's Presence that I felt so strongly earlier, praying about Anne and what was amiss. I was given an immediate answer. Upon looking back up at her, there was no doubt about it – she had been crying before I entered her office.

At first, I didn't ask any questions, trying not to pry. I stayed focused on the work that was in front of us, being mindful of the time constraints that were upon us. But as I was sitting there, I kept having this overwhelming push to question what was wrong.

I finally gave in to the realization that something was definitely not right. She appeared to be quite sorrowful. I gently inquired if everything was okay with her.

She stopped entering the figures into her documents, slowly laid down her pencil on the stack of papers in front of her, and stared down at her hands. Immediately, she was digging for tissues as tears were filling her eyes. Anne took a sip of water and dabbed her cheeks before uttering a word. I could tell that whatever was bothering her was difficult for her to talk about.

Her voice quivered as she started to tell me that not that many hours before our appointment, she learned that her sister had Stage IV blood cancer. The doctors were giving her a maximum of two years to live.

Anne cried, "To make matters worse, she is an atheist."

Anne continued shedding multiple tears while speaking, saying that she was losing all hope that something positive might come from this situation. She revealed that a terminal diagnosis would be less frightening if her sister was a Christian. Because she could then be more confident about where she was going when she passed from this life. However, this was not the case, and to make things worse, she was not approachable regarding matters of faith. Anne stated that her sister viewed Christians as weak. From her perspective, people like us use Jesus as a crutch in life.

Hearing Anne say those words caught me much by surprise. I've never heard that viewpoint articulated quite that way before. It really made my heart sink to hear that someone could view Jesus and Christianity in that way.

In my opinion, following Christ takes more courage than the other way around. But I didn't say anything outright, because I knew that Anne already knew that this concept was misguided. Through our conversations over the years, Anne's faith in Jesus was evident. She was merely highlighting the seriousness of the situation surrounding her sister.

Anne elaborated on the details, stating that her sister never knew she was sick until her spine started fracturing on its own. This predicament prompted the doctors to schedule immediate surgery. The plan was to perform a spinal fusion that would permanently connect those broken vertebrae back together. During her time in rehab following the operation, she was informed of the severe and detrimental nature of her condition.

I discovered that her sister turned down all the options that were available to treat the cancer once she understood the seriousness and gravity of the disease. Anne believed that her sister's refusal to receive treatment was a result of her undoubtedly thinking, "Why should she?"

Anne thought her sister's perspective was that she came from dust and would return to dust, so there was no real value in continuing to live anyway. According to her, her sister had simply accepted the prognosis she was facing and was preparing for the end of her life.

Anne revealed that she is the only Believer in her family. Her prayer right then was for her sister to discover God and understand His realness.

As Anne quietly wept, trying to control her sadness, I broke through the heaviness in the room. I asked her, "Anne, don't you remember what I have written about? Do you not remember some of the miracle stories I have witnessed and shared with you previously? That doctor in Ohio? Dr. Nemeh? And all the miracles that surround this man?"

Anne cracked a small smile, but then it disappeared quickly. She shook her head, sighing dejectedly, revealing, "No, my sister would NEVER go or have him pray or anything like that. She doesn't believe and thinks we are weak to believe in a God. She is obsessed with being in control and believes that this is the end of life. Period."

It was evident that Anne had attempted to have faith-based conversations with her sister in the past. She was aware that persuasion was not enough to overcome her sister's many misconceptions. I conceded and left well enough alone. She was already going through a difficult time.

I offered to send Dr. Nemeh her sister's name via email. I also communicated that we had a trip coming up in March to see him. I suggested that we bring a photo for him to pray over in person, too. She would just have to provide me with one so I could do this for her. The sadness of the situation still consumed Anne, but the small glimpse of hope that was just offered moved her heart.

Anne understood that the timing of me being there just when she learned about her sister's condition was not a coincidence. Had she known about these circumstances earlier, even just a day or two earlier, I wouldn't have noticed the immense sadness and asked any questions. And likewise, there is no way I could have ever found out about it if it were later. The arrangement for me to be present at that particular time was perfect. There was no doubt that God was behind it.

Ecclesiastes 3:1

There is a time for everything.

six.

EVERYTHING WILL BE OKAY

Anne and I spent the next two hours in deep conversation. We spoke about the various ways that God worked His way into her life and how she came to believe in Jesus. She was like me and grew up without faith in her childhood home. Still, God continuously worked on reaching Anne, until she became aware of the numerous signs that He was giving her. She shared some significant moments throughout her life that God used to help her get there.

One of which was quite extraordinary. Anne told me a story about one remarkable event that helped her receive comfort and later was used to strengthen her faith. It happened on a special day, her daughter's birthday. Anne was planning to travel the two-hour drive to be with her and celebrate. Anne remembers it being a beautiful, sunny day. She was very excited to see her daughter and had made a great effort to plan ahead for this special occasion.

She recalled nearly halfway into the drive, that she was following a semitruck that apparently was reflecting the sun's bright rays, bouncing them in her direction, until the light landed on her. For miles she followed that truck, and even though the light was not blinding, she noticed that it was continually there.

After a while, she decided to pass the vehicle. After doing so, she glanced in her rearview mirror to look back. She could see the truck that she had just passed, but then she noticed that the light hadn't moved. It was still presently touching down on her.

Instantly, she knew that was odd. A few seconds later when she was trying to determine where it was coming from, something caught her attention and made her head turn to the left.

There next to her car was an angel of light. It traveled steadily and brilliantly alongside her car. She couldn't believe her eyes. Right then, the angel spoke to her heart, and she heard, "Everything will be okay."

It stared at her for a few seconds more, and then just like that, the angel departed. Anne said watching it leave was also something that stood out vividly in her memory, saying that it was like the angel went through a pass or an opening, then turned a corner, and then vanished.

Anne replayed in her mind what the angel said, but in the form of a question, *Everything will be okay?*

She wondered, *What did that mean?*

She started to worry that maybe something was wrong with one of her family members. Immediately she phoned both of her daughters, her spouse, everyone she could think of, to check on their well-being. She was relieved to find out that everyone she contacted was safe and doing well. Even so, she didn't know what to make of this statement. It left her feeling anxious and bewildered.

Shortly after arriving at her daughter's apartment, she received a phone call that shed some light on that angelic message. She heard that the building where she leased her office space from was going up in flames. Fire crews were battling the fire, but things didn't look so good for her office.

Once she disconnected the call, all sorts of emotions began stirring inside herself. She knew she would have to change her plans and head back home, but then came the recognition of what happened earlier. Anne suddenly viewed that message differently. Now she saw it as a message of compassion. God wanted her to know that even though something bad was occurring, He was watching over her.

Anne was trying her best to trust that everything really would be okay as her mind raced to what it would mean for her and her clients if she lost everything in that fire. Computers, tax records, and decades of paperwork were among those things that could now be lying in a rubble of ashes. Her heart sank just at the thought of what may be waiting for her when she got back to town.

She arrived at her office, relieved to note that even though it was seriously burned, there still remained a structure standing in front of her. Her eyes surveyed the long line of barricade tape that was there to promote safety by blocking admittance into any part of the building. She wanted to go in and have a look around but knew that was not wise nor permitted. Luckily, someone asked her what she was hoping to find, if they could arrange for some of the emergency workers to have a look for her.

Anne reported stacks of checks and reports she had left there, along with the exact location of where they could find them in the office. Several officials went in and were amazed to find the items inside floating on a shelf. They were dry and miraculously unharmed. Not only did the fire not touch them, but the fire sprinkler system also missed them as well. The individual who grabbed her things looked up and realized how this came to be. The drop-out ceiling system installed in that building was positioned beneath the fire sprinklers. Normally when exposed to heat from a fire, the panels would soften and fall from the metal grid onto the ground.

For some unknown reason, the ceiling panel directly above everything Anne so desperately needed to be rescued, became dysfunctional and never dropped. Instead of softening and falling out, it remained intact, and elongating itself to stretch beyond its normal capacity. Therefore, it stood in place during the blaze, catching gallons of water that had fallen from the sprinkler directly above. It was under immense weight, looking like it was about to let loose at any moment.

The officers quickly grabbed her items along with her computers that were also somehow unscathed. They made their thoughts known to Anne, declaring "Boy, someone was watching over you today."

Anne smiled and said, "Yes, *SOMEONE* sure was."

Anne recounted other instances where God had given her clear-cut messages to reveal Himself and bring her closer to Him. To this day, she pays close attention to the ways God communicates to her, not wanting to miss a single one.

After we finished talking and wrapped up our tax session, I left reminding Anne I would reach out to Dr. Nemeh's wife Kathy, asking for prayers for her sister.

Leaving her office, I was thinking about my day thus far. How it began with the doves and then the conversation that Anne and

I had with each other. I felt sad for what Anne was going through over worrying for her sister. As I rode the elevator down to the first floor, I remembered I had been hauling extra copies of the books in my car that I recently wrote and mentioned to her, *The Power of God... Today,* and *The Power of God... Tomorrow.* After grabbing one of each, I returned to the new building where Anne was currently working, ever since that devastating fire years ago.

I proceeded my way through the lobby towards the elevator. As I approached, and practically close enough that I could push the "up" button to return back to the fourth floor where Anne's office was, the elevator doors opened up all on their own. No one was inside so I hopped in, thinking that was strange. Observing that likewise, none of the floor designator buttons inside were lit up either made me think maybe this was God's way of letting me know that He was right there with me.

"That was neat!" I whispered to myself.

I ran the books up to Anne, telling her I wanted her to have them. I gave her a big hug and reminded her that I wouldn't forget the promise I made about giving her sister's name to Dr. Nemeh. She became teary-eyed again.

In a quiet voice she thanked me and said that she now had hope. A hope that wasn't there before.

Psalms 121:5-8 NIV

The LORD watches over you— the LORD is your shade at your right hand; the sun will not harm you by day, nor the moon by night. The LORD will keep you from all harm— he will watch over your life; the LORD will watch over your coming and going both now and forevermore.

seven.

STUPEFIED

I got a phone call from Anne on Thursday morning, February 23rd. I heard her crying when I answered, "Hello?"

At first, when I saw the call coming in, I assumed she was calling to give me an update on my taxes. As soon as I pressed the phone to my ear, I knew there was another reason.

My heart raced instantly, and I became somewhat frightened to inquire about the matter.

Anne was the first to speak, posing a question: "Christine, you mentioned that you would give that doctor my sister's name."

I froze and felt my body tighten. I answered, "Uh huh."

Anne asked another question, "Did you do that? Did you give him her name?"

I became nervous by this line of questioning, especially considering I believed I had heard her crying when I picked up my phone.

I had a suspicion that something had changed, but I wasn't sure what it was. *Maybe her sister has gotten worse?* I worried.

I quickly shook that terrible thought from my mind. I made a commitment to tell her the truth of the matter while waiting for her to provide more details.

"Yes, I did Anne. That day, I went straight home and sent an email to his wife, Kathy Nemeh. She assured me that they would be offering prayers for her."

Anne exhaled with a heavy sigh. There was a delay in her reply. I felt anxious and jittery as I nervously awaited to hear what was happening.

I heard Anne whisper, "I thought that's what happened."

By now, my mind was overly focused, and I was thinking about the worst-case scenarios: *Did God not answer our prayers? Was there a worsening with her sister's situation?*

Anne interrupted my negative thoughts that were spiraling downward and informed me that her sister had just called her a little bit ago. When Anne answered the call, she said she knew something was up because her sister's voice was upbeat. Then her sister announced, "I have wonderful news!"

"The doctors are stupefied and baffled as to how they could have misdiagnosed me the way they did."

Anne sat silently, listening to her sister joyfully describing the news. Now, the doctors were thinking she only had some blood disorder that was affecting only nine percent of her total blood cells.

Anne questioned her sister, "And what about the other ninety-one percent? Are they all okay, then?"

Her sister, amused by Anne's rapid draw on figures, laughed and, said, "Yeah, I guess so."

She kept repeating that the doctors used the word "stupefied." They were absolutely puzzled as to how they could have been so wrong.

Anne reassured me, "But I know what happened. There was no misdiagnosis at all! God healed her!"

She was elated. The quiet sobs I heard over the phone this time were from her delighting in this beautiful miracle that God had just given.

After our phone call, I sent an email to Kathy Nemeh. Tears filled my eyes as I typed up the details surrounding this sudden and incredible improvement in Anne's sister. Kathy wrote back, thrilled with the news, adding, "Your friend, Anne, should inform her sister about what happened."

When I reported to Anne of Kathy's advice, she reiterated what she said before, that she just could not speak with her sister about this sort of thing. Anne stressed, "She would laugh it off, chalking it up to only being a coincidence, and remind me how weak I was to believe in such nonsensical things."

Anne was not giving up, however. She would continue praying that this health crisis would not go unnoticed. She was optimistic that one day God would touch her sister, bringing her to the realization that we are connected to something much larger than ourselves.

I had a great deal of sympathy for Anne. Knowing her sister didn't believe in God was painful for Anne, and I knew that she wished she could speak to her about it. Her best option was to pray that God would change her sister's heart and open her eyes to the truth. Especially considering her sister was unwilling to listen. Meanwhile, Anne is actually witnessing the Gospel to her sister, just by living out her Christian life in front of her. In the end, Anne was relying on God's power and grace to save her sister.

It seems to me that nearly every Christian has someone they know and care about who does not believe. Or they are aware of someone who has walked away from practicing a love for God in their daily living. It's not easy to watch and observe, that's for sure.

There are a few people in our family who fall into these categories.

One person who I noticed walking away was my oldest daughter, Collette. I was unaware of it until her latter college years. I wanted to say something but never did. I'm hesitant to discuss anything that could cause conflict between me and someone I deeply love because of the many losses I've dealt with throughout my life. I am certain that she would have been open to talking about it, but I couldn't bring myself to inquire about her convictions at that time.

Our faith and beliefs are something Collette is familiar with, still, it has been a topic that has been left unaddressed and avoided by both parties over the years. Slowly, I began to observe that she was unwilling to participate in the prayers she had been accustomed to during her childhood, such as the blessing before our meals. Despite the heartbreaking nature of this, I continued to steer clear of the topic, just as she did. It was just something that went by unspoken for years.

After God changed our lives so dramatically back in 2019, Emily and I informed Collette about our own set of miracles and the way God was healing not just us but so many others. To help her understand more, I gifted Collette a copy of my first book, *The Power of God... Today*. I was astonished to discover that she had actually read it, especially since it was beyond her usual interests. The fact that she was willing to do so deeply moved my heart.

She told me that she enjoyed reading it. I was hoping that her reading the book would initiate a conversation about the miracle stories she read about, but it didn't really. We had a few brief discussions but nothing that was particularly profound. Collette's perception of God didn't seem to change either. Nonetheless, I had faith that God would reveal Himself to her at the right time.

Recently, I have made efforts to converse more frequently about faith matters with Collette, but tackling the subject has always been challenging for me. Ironically, opening my heart and discussing my relationship with Christ with a stranger is often easier than talking to those closest to me.

I usually ask the Holy Spirit for guidance on when or if to speak since Collette has never asked me a question on her own about God. And if I do speak, I try to take small steps and make my mentions short and sweet. Whenever I thought it was appropriate to do so, she has always been respectful and attentive. I am certain that there were instances when she was not all that interested or may have easily dismissed a miracle story I shared as only a coincidence. But that wasn't a problem for me.

I was making use of those brief moments to try and incorporate her into my world. I remained optimistic that sharing some of these stories, which I cherish with all my heart, would eventually have a positive effect on her in the process. Meanwhile, I continue praying tirelessly for her, day and night, hoping that the Lord will manifest Himself in the particular way that she needs. I am confident that she will one day find Him.

Psalm 31:24
Be strong and take heart,
all you who hope in the Lord.

eight.

JESUS IS A GENTLEMAN

Shortly after discovering the miracle that God performed for Anne's sister, Collette, Emily and I had planned an entire weekend together in West Des Moines, Iowa. Every year, the three of us take a road trip to a nearby destination as a mother-daughter getaway. These trips are wonderful because they forge and strengthen our relationships with one another while also creating beautiful memories at the same time.

On this occasion, however, I had been guided to introduce Collette to a different yet similar matter that I rarely spoke about by giving her another book to read. It was not something I wrote. Instead, it was a book I discovered while dusting and organizing my bookshelves one day. I picked it up, recognizing that I had purchased it years ago but had never read it.

Upon examining the title *Imagine Heaven: Near-Death Experiences, God's Promises, and the Exhilarating Future That Awaits You* by author John Burke, I was intrigued. I began to read it and couldn't put it down. This was not a wacky pie in the sky type of book. Instead, it was a well-researched one that incorporated more than one thousand near-death experiences (NDEs) that pointed to the reality of what awaits us after this life. I found this book to be one of the most impactful books I have ever read.

Since Collette's first degree is a bachelor's in chemical engineering, and this author similarly had an analytical mind, studied engineering, and used to be a skeptic himself, I thought that she might be able to relate to his conclusions. The author explains how he became a believer in God through NDE stories like the ones assembled in his book. He spent hundreds of hours analyzing and reviewing them. All of which directed him to identify the commonality among most of them that perfectly aligned with the Heaven that is promised in Scripture.

There were stories of blind people who had never seen anything their entire lives, who died and came back, reporting their experiences in Heaven with perfect clarity. There are many documented reports by those who had more to gain by staying silent than by sharing their encounters with the public. People such as doctors, lawyers, pilots, and even many from other religions. The author also mentions that in the United States, almost one in twenty-five individuals have had a near-death experience. It is believed that it is more common in Europe, with statistical data indicating that one in ten people have had one. Stories like these are reported by millions of people worldwide, most of which have the same common theme that God is real and Heaven truly exists.

Over the course of the weekend, I prayed for the best time to give this book to her. I was made aware to wait it out for a night, leading me to set my goal for Saturday evening. Sure enough, the conditions to give it to her that evening were perfect.

The three of us gathered together on the couch in our hotel suite and conversed about many things. The discussion was not just about personal issues but also about the moral aspects of our lives. I was able to use this subject matter as a perfect platform to add that I had a gift for each of them. I hurried back into the bedroom to get the book. Throughout the process, I was praying that God would provide me with the right words to introduce the subject to her.

I was hoping that Collette's reaction would be favorable, and it was. When I handed the book over, Collette genuinely expressed interest in why I had chosen that book in particular. This question of hers presented an excellent opportunity for us to have a meaningful discussion revolving around all aspects of faith, including atheism and skepticism versus believing in God and Heaven. We even talked about my father and why I believed he remained uncertain about God's existence throughout his life. I stressed to her that all it takes for God to reveal Himself to someone is that they are willing to open their hearts to Him, even if it's just a little.

"All Jesus needs is a crack," I told her. "He is a gentleman and will not budge His way in. He will wait for you to invite Him in first."

Collette made note of the funny timing, revealing that she had recently been drawn to cathedrals and churches while traveling overseas. Despite being quick to point out that she believed the reasons behind it were more due to her interest in architecture than anything else. Still, she found her newfound fascination with them to be curious and she would often go inside for a peek. Our conversation lasted until the late hours of the night, until we finally decided to call it a day.

As usual, I silently prayed for all my children as I went to sleep. But this time, I was explicitly asking God to work on softening Collette's heart. I had a strong desire for her to witness the beauty of believing in Christ and hoped she would be willing to respond.

The following morning, I woke up believing that the conversations the night before had enabled Collette to draw a little closer to God than she was previously.

I was brave enough to trust my feelings and asked Collette if she wanted to join Emily and me for Mass that morning. There was a short, awkward pause, but then she tepidly agreed. I was trying to play it cool by nodding my head and smiling, but I had a deep desire to jump up and down for joy. I knew that her willingness to go with us was a huge sign of her beginning to open up, even if only a little bit.

We found a church nearby that was only a short ten-minute drive away. The church was packed with lots of young families. Even though our pew was a bit crowded, it was still a pleasant sight. Despite Emily sitting between us, I was still able to see Collette from the corner of my eye. From her overall demeanor, it seemed like she found the experience of attending Mass again mostly enjoyable. Occasionally, however, I would observe her appearing uneasy by crossing her arms and indicating a desire to leave.

I was uncertain if she was aware of the internal struggle that seemed to be taking place, but I noticed it. As a child, she grew up with our family attending Mass every Sunday. Her adult years is when she decided to take a step back, appearing to be uncertain about God's existence. I have never felt hostility towards the

Church from Collette, and honestly, I don't truly know what is in her heart because I haven't asked. I was concerned that if I did, I might hear words that could potentially break my heart. I simply pray and trust that Jesus hears my daily prayers for her.

Once Mass was over and we were walking out to the car, Emily's phone went off. As she slipped it out of her pocket, she noticed that she had just received a text from a good friend of hers. This friend is quite a prayer warrior. His name is Graeson Dall. He and Emily met years earlier. They were introduced by a mutual friend who knew their lives had both recently and drastically changed due to Jesus stepping into their lives in tremendous ways. The mutual friend thought introducing them would be advantageous since they were around the same age and could relate to each other's spiritual journey.

Graeson's life story can be accessed through YouTube or Googling him. His walk with Christ is a source of inspiration for individuals of all ages, particularly since he is a young man in his mid-twenties who is completely devoted to Christ. He belongs to an organization called *Prairie Fire Ministries*. They hold monthly healing services at the cathedral in Des Moines, Iowa, and are expanding to other cities and states as well.

Graeson sent Emily a text because he had spotted us during Mass. He attempted to find us afterwards to say a quick "hello," but we had already left. He remained inside and stated that he would love to chat with us if we had a moment.

Collette was almost ready to go home because our weekend getaway was coming to an end. Regardless, she was willing to take a few extra minutes out of our busy schedule to meet this young man we were so fond of. The three of us did an about-face and returned to the gathering space just inside the church's main doors, where Graeson stood. He came over and greeted Emily and me with a hug '*hello*.' Then, his eyes landed on Collette.

Collette's attention seemed to be instantly captivated by Graeson's quick charm and smile. Collette had no knowledge of Graeson's background, but we were well aware that he was not just your typical average young man. From a young age, the Lord has had a special calling on his life. Graeson is often inspired by the Holy Spirit to speak words that someone needs to hear, or he will automatically be enlightened about specific struggles in that person's life. It is seen with Graeson's unjudging heart to help guide him on what to say or how to pray for that particular individual. Graeson follows the Lord's promptings, hoping his words or knowledge will help bring that individual closer to Jesus.

As we stood there smiling at each other as if it were by chance that we met him in this parish, it became apparent that this meeting was not an accident. God hears our prayers.

As we introduced Collette and informed him about our girl's trip, Graeson greeted her with a cheerful smile. He stared at her briefly, then enthusiastically asked us, "Hey, do you guys want to pray?"

He kept his eyes on Collette. At first, Collette smiled nervously and then she laughed a little. She glanced at Emily and me, observing our facial reactions to the question at hand. We were both nodding in agreement, indicating our willingness to comply with his request.

Collette finally replied, "Sure?"

Her response was more like a question than an answer.

Graeson quickly obtained approval from one of the priests to bring us into the church's nave. He moved four chairs in a circle in a space close to the Tabernacle. After that, he concentrated solely on Collette.

Graeson began by asking Collette if she had been baptized. She had been. On March 21st, 1997, my three older children, Collette, Joshua, Matthew, and I, were all baptized together on the same day with Randy standing there beside us.

Next, Graeson inquired if he could pray a blessing over her life. He also wanted to know if she had a desire for Jesus to enter her life. Collette responded, "Yes."

Despite the tears forming in my eyes when she said "yes," I knew to push through any emotions that came to me. This beautiful moment was all about Collette and her relationship with Jesus. Graeson requested that Collette bow her head and open her hands as if she were receiving a gift.

While Emily and I silently prayed with him, he prayed the most beautiful words over my daughter. After that, Graeson informed her that from now on, whenever she is traveling and visiting churches, she will smell roses. It would be God's way of showing her that He was truly present.

Graeson explained that there are many misconceptions about living a Christian life. He asserted that it is actually one of the most beautiful ways to live. "There is no greater love than to lay down your life for a friend, so we, in turn, surrender our lives over to Christ because He died for us."

He informed her that God only desired the best for her life, and the fastest path to securing the best life is through Him.

Graeson continued, "You give Jesus a crack, just a sliver… an inch, and He will come into your life. But He waits for us to choose Him first. He won't barge His way in. He is a gentleman."

I noted that the words he used were strangely similar to the ones I used the night before and were having a significant impact on her. The tears that formed in her eyes spoke volumes. After Graeson finished, he mentioned that he needed to go. We hugged him and expressed our gratitude for his time and prayers. Collette thanked him, too, but she was still feeling a bit of shock about what had just happened.

As we returned to the car, I asked Collette if she'd be interested in taking a walk. I had a feeling that we needed to stay and make the most of this special moment. I pointed out that we could simply leave our car at the church parking lot and begin from there. She agreed that it sounded like a good idea.

We took out our hats and gloves from the trunk and started walking. Collette recounted the strange and extraordinary experience of running into this Graeson fellow. She couldn't believe how he touched on the same topics we had just discussed the night before. Furthermore, he told her that when traveling and visiting a church, she would smell roses. Churches that she just mentioned the night before that she had been visiting while on business in other countries. She knew there was no way Graeson could have known about any of that all on his own.

Graeson echoed my sentiment that Jesus was a gentleman, and stated, "He waits to be invited in."

She kept reiterating how wild and peculiar that all was. One of Collette's last comments that left us in laughter was that no matter what, even if she wanted to, she couldn't forget her remarkable encounter with our good friend Graeson Dall.

Matthew 18:12-14

"What do you think? If a man owns a hundred sheep, and one of them wanders away, will he not leave the ninety-nine on the hills and go to look for the one that wandered off? And if he finds it, truly I tell you, he is happier about that one sheep than about the ninety-nine that did not wander off. In the same way your Father in heaven is not willing that any of these little ones should perish."

nine.

SWEET DREAMS

My life has been blessed by Graeson on many occasions. The previous time, it was for another family member, my second-oldest child, Josh. As his mother, I had an uneasy feeling that something wasn't right with him, but I was unable to pinpoint the cause. I tried to ignore the feeling and shrug it off, but I kept feeling a gnawing sensation in my spirit that Josh was in trouble. Everything seemed to be fine on the surface, but I was still extremely concerned even though I couldn't determine what was causing the issue.

Over the years, Josh has made some minor detours from his faith, taking some side paths along the way. Ultimately, he never lost his faith in the Lord despite the many twists and turns he encountered. It was common for Josh to join me and Emily for different faith-filled events. His faith and the love of the Lord would be evident every time. However, it never failed. These spiritual highs were always short-lived, and he would eventually lose his passion and return to things of the world. It was heart-wrenching to watch.

It was like I was witnessing the story of the seed being sown on the rocky ground unfold repeatedly in front of me. Initially, the seed, which had Jesus and the Holy Spirit living inside of him, began to flourish with much enthusiasm, but it didn't penetrate deep enough to take root. As Josh circled and moved in the opposite direction again, his attraction to the Christian lifestyle would begin to fade away.

This matter had been bothering me for months. The realization that something was seriously wrong and the feeling of being unable to do anything was starting to take its toll on me. I had been praying the whole time, but recently it seemed more urgent that something had to be done. On August 9th, 2022, I had a desperate conversation with Jesus about my son and prayed for a way to reach him. Shortly after this, I came across the Miracle Prayer card that I had received from Dr. Nemeh's healing service years ago. I had kept every item I received from those prayer services we attended so long ago.

When I came across it that night, I was amazed at the timing and the fact that I had forgotten about having it. I picked it up, carefully studying the card. A colored image of our Lord is displayed on the front of the card. While carrying His Cross, His Beautiful Sacred Heart is clearly visible with His eyes lowered.

This lovely prayer is located on the backside:

The Miracle Prayer
Lord Jesus, I come before You, just as I am; I am sorry for my sins, I repent of my sins, please forgive me. In Your Name, I forgive all others for what they have done against me. I renounce Satan, the evil spirits and all their works. I give You my entire self, Lord Jesus; I accept You as my Lord, God, and Savior. Heal me, change me, strengthen me in body, soul, and spirit.
Come Lord Jesus, cover me with Your Precious Blood and fill me with Your Holy Spirit. I love You Lord Jesus, I praise You Lord Jesus, I thank You Lord Jesus; I shall follow You every day of my life.
Mary, my Mother, Queen of Peace, and all you angels and saints, please help me. Amen.

I burst into tears, and before I knew it, I was crying hard. I began to pray with all the love and hope I had for my son as my tears flowed uncontrollably. I gave Jesus everything I had, all my worries and concerns. After I had finished handing it over, I dried my eyes and calmed my mind. I managed to regain my composure and finish a few necessary tasks before going to bed for the evening. As I climbed into bed, my tears started again. The walls echoed with my sobs before I finally drifted off to sleep that night.

I was astonished by what transpired next. As I slept with my rosary, special prayer card, and many tissues and tears, I was given a remarkable prophetic dream that would detail the next day. I was given a clear depiction of how God would step in and assist my son.

The dream began with me visiting Josh at his house. The two of us were sitting on his front step, discussing exactly what had been on my heart for a while. I conveyed to him that I could sense that he was experiencing some significant problems in his life, and that he was in a poor spiritual state. I revealed to him that I could literally see it.

He quickly shot me a look and asked how to see such a thing was possible. I explained that the Holy Spirit gives me certain signs, and I just knew. He was obviously upset by my comment and insisted that I refrain from saying such things.

So, then, I asked him, "Well, how do you think you are doing?"

He said he wanted to figure out his life and learn how to live differently.

I smiled at his profound statement, saying there was a spiritual healing waiting for him. His eyes were filled with curiosity as he looked up at me. Expounding on that mysterious statement, I added, "All that you have to do, Josh, is surrender to what God wants for your life. You must trust Him with what He has for you."

Josh was attentive, listening carefully, and I sensed a change in Josh's inner state just from hearing those words.

I made it clear to him that Emily, his sister, had been praying for him, and she also asked our friend Graeson to pray for him, too. Graeson had only been mentioned to Josh at this point, he had never had the chance to meet him before.

While still dreaming, I gave Josh information about an upcoming Healing Service that Graeson and his ministry were holding in Des Moines on an upcoming Wednesday evening. Josh briefly mentioned that he was worried that if we went, we would return home extremely late, because he had to wake up at the crack of dawn for work. Nevertheless, he was willing to attend this event with us, meet Graeson, and talk to him about his situation.

As the dream continued, Emily and I drove Josh to the Healing Service days later. Josh met Graeson, and Graeson prayed for him. I witnessed God healing Josh's soul, but the best part was that I was told that everything God did for him would never leave. I was shown that Josh would always be deeply connected to Christ after this experience.

I woke up utterly shocked from this amazing dream at the peak of the three o'clock hour, which is "The Hour of Great Mercy." Our Lord died on the cross for our redemption at this hour. At 3:00 p.m. on Good Friday, Jesus breathed out his last breath and said, "Father, into thy hands I commend my spirit." Luke 23:46.

Many Christians believe that Jesus attaches special significance to this hour. Right then, I was prompted to begin praying the Divine Mercy Chaplet for my son. I begged for Jesus' mercy to be extended to my son and for God to be able to reach him. After I had completed my prayer, I asked the Holy Spirit for assistance in interpreting the dream. Within an instant, God made it clear to me that I should drive over to Josh's place the next morning. I was even informed of the precise time I needed to arrive. I was to be there at 10:00 a.m. sharp. Additionally, I had a clear understanding that I would have the exact same conversation that was just revealed to me in this dream.

I was aware that everything that took place in that dream would come to pass. I rested in the knowledge that God would take care of Josh. Despite everything, I managed to get back to sleep and woke up several hours later. I knew that my mission was to help Josh prepare for what God had in store. I thanked God abundantly for hearing my prayers and giving me great hope for what was to come.

Jeremiah 33:3

Call to me and I will answer you and tell you great and unsearchable things you do not know.

ten.

SPIRITUAL SENSE

I arose from bed, still completely awed by what had happened in the dream and what I sensed the Holy Spirit had conveyed to me. I retrieved my phone to confirm the healing service I was instructed to take Josh to was still scheduled. I was shocked to learn it was only a few days away. I was aware that I had to trust what was presented and follow through. Rushing into Emily's room, I woke her up and provided her with a detailed account of my night. She was covered in goosebumps when learning about the sequence of events.

When leaving her room, I realized that I had a lot of things to do before the divine appointment at ten o'clock, which was only a few hours away. I knew that was the precise moment I was to be knocking on Josh's front door.

Josh usually wakes up extremely early in the morning to go to work, so Emily asked a question I hadn't even considered, "But, Mom, what if he's not at home?"

I stopped and paused for a minute but then quickly dismissed the concern. Confidentially, I replied, "Don't worry, he will be. His days and nights have been a bit mixed up the past few days anyway."

A few minutes later, Emily was eating breakfast and posed another alarming question. Her inquiry was based on a very real possibility, particularly due to Josh's reputation for being a heavy sleeper. In the past, we have previously joked that he could sleep through a train wreck without hearing a sound. Consequently, Emily wanted to know, "But, Mom, have you thought about what happens if he doesn't wake up?"

I had so much faith in what God had shown me that I just smiled and said, "I know he will, honey. This is an answer to my prayers last night."

As Emily left for work, I kissed her goodbye, wished her a wonderful day, and assured her that I would keep her informed. I was confident that she would be praying with me to ensure that everything would go as planned. Hurriedly and excitedly, I finished a few chores, got ready, and drove the twenty-some minutes to Josh's house. As soon as I turned onto his street, I noticed his truck in the driveway. "Wow, he WAS home!" I said, praying as I pulled in behind him.

I checked the time on my dash and saw that it was 9:52 a.m., which meant I had eight more minutes to wait. Being that my son is very independent, I was worried that he wouldn't be too thrilled to see me there, trying to help him through a tough period in his life. So, I used my time wisely. I sat there, praying and praying. Praying for the Holy Spirit to be with both of us. Praying that I would be enlightened about what to say and be able to speak with boldness.

I confidently stepped out of my car at 9:58 a.m., taking deep breaths as I approached Josh's front steps. I raised my hand, paused momentarily, then finally knocked on the door and waited. No answer.

My heart was pounding hard. I sighed. I made another attempt. This time, success! Josh cautiously glanced out the door. It was evident that he had just woken up. When he realized it was me, he stood there with a puzzled look on his face and asked in a sleepy tone what was going on. I informed him that I needed to speak with him.

What I just said seemed to make Josh feel uneasy. He stood and stared at me, clearing his throat and rubbing the back of his neck. He glanced behind himself and then turned to me, saying he needed a moment. He mentioned that his house was messy, and he would come out on the front step and converse with me there.

I stepped away while he shut the door. *Wow,* I thought, *just like in my dream!*

He stepped outside a few minutes later, and we sat side by side on his front step.

Josh looked up at me with concern, asking, "What's up?"

I let him know that everything was alright, but I needed to talk to him.

He turned his eyes towards the ground. He uttered, "Okaayy," with a quick, nervous laugh.

I silently called out to God for help. I slowly revealed my reason for being there. I started out by telling him that I could see he was having some troubles. I knew that he was not in a good place spiritually. I revealed to him that I could literally see it.

He gave me a quick, annoyed glance and asked how it was possible to see such a thing. I explained there were certain signs that the Holy Spirit gives me, and I just knew. And just like in the dream, he became upset by my comment, insisting that I shouldn't say such things. I informed him that Dr. Nemeh taught me that when someone walks in the Spirit, they possess more than just the usual five physical senses. And because of this truth, I had been given the ability of knowing, and even seeing, that he was not doing so well spiritually speaking.

Our conversation was the same as the one I had with him in my dream the night before, almost word for word. It was completely unbelievable! Josh agreed to attend the healing service to receive prayer and was deeply touched by my concerns for him. He acknowledged that he wasn't in a good place right now and could certainly benefit from some prayers.

Josh admitted that he was going through one of the most difficult times of his life. I could see the pain in his eyes when he spoke. The conversation was emotional and lasted for over an hour. We discussed everything in great detail and talked extensively about our physical lives versus the one that is more significant, our spiritual lives.

Throughout our conversation, we both shed a few tears. Josh pulled back and stared at me intently for a moment before offering a heartfelt "thank you."

As I turned to leave, Josh laughed while announcing that he wouldn't have woken up if it weren't for me rattling the doorknob.

"You rattling the doorknob like that, AND THEN trying to push the door open, that was what woke me up! I was wondering, *Who is trying to come inside my house*?"

I stopped, turned around, and inspected Josh's face to see if he was attempting to be humorous with me. There was nothing. He was serious.

"Josh, that wasn't me. I just knocked."

Josh looked stunned. He said, "What do you mean, that wasn't you? I woke up because I heard you struggling with the doorknob and trying to get in. I was confused by it and wondering *who in the world was trying to break into my house*!"

At that point, I gained clarity. Repeating myself, "Josh, I only knocked."

I waited for him to get it while we stared at each other for a minute. He didn't. He was totally confused by what I said and what he believed he heard.

"Josh, I am pretty sure I know what happened here."

"What is that?" he asked.

"Jesus helped me out," I claimed.

Josh was taken aback by my comment. He continued trying to process, "Are you sure? ...I mean, that you didn't try to come in?"

"Yes, I am one hundred percent sure. I trusted that you would answer the door, given that God had inspired and led me here by giving me that dream I told you about. He had laid out everything for me, including our entire conversation, what time I should show up, and even where we would be sitting. I was confident that you would come to the door, so all I did was knock and wait. Even little miracles like that are a common occurrence when we walk in faith with our Lord."

We stared at each other for another minute while Josh was still processing. Then, I decided to walk back over to him and give him a few pieces of advice before leaving. The healing service that I was told to take Josh to and that he agreed to attend was coming up in seven days. I recommended that he prepare himself well. I suggested a number of measures, including reading Scripture, praying more, and asking for assistance from those in Heaven. I reminded him that my mother, his grandmother, was also there in Heaven to pray for him.

I advised him to capture his thoughts and make them conform to Christ. I said, "Work hard and accept this challenge to get your soul into shape," to which he laughed.

I continued my instruction, "You NEED to activate your faith. Work on it for the next seven days before the service."

Josh acknowledged that he felt God calling him in various ways in life, but he always had a fear of what that meant. Frequently, it would produce the opposite outcome, and he would end up running away from it instead of moving towards it. He declared, "I don't know. Sometimes I don't want to listen. I just want to do my own thing."

In a casual manner, I mentioned, "That's what Lucifer wanted to do, too…to do his own thing."

Josh scoffed at my words, and I felt immediate regret, realizing it was a completely unfair comparison.

I gave him another hug, and we both laughed. "I am sorry," I said, apologizing for the harsh words I used.

I tried to make amends by saying, "Josh, you know, I would give up my life for you in a second if I had to."

This true but off-the-wall statement made Josh burst out laughing, to which he said, "Well, I sure hope that doesn't have to happen."

After he had a good laugh, Josh quickly became serious and said that there was something else bothering him lately. He mentioned that everyone he encountered recently seemed to have concern for him and his welfare, even casual acquaintances, and it really agitated him.

"I know it shouldn't. They are just being nice. But I don't get it. Why is everyone so concerned for me? It drives me crazy!"

Before I could even contemplate what to say, I heard myself speak, "I know why everyone is concerned. God has a purpose for your life, and He is making use of those around you to guide you towards it. We are all part of God's family, and family looks out for one another."

"Josh, I'm not entirely sure what your calling is or where it will lead you. It may have to do with reaching the lost...especially to those who most people are not so inclined to assist. God will use your background and all the hardships you've faced to guide and bless others if you allow Him."

"Only if you allow Him. Begin to allow Jesus in by opening up your heart, even if it's just a small crack at first."

We were both in tears when I left to go attend the noon Mass in Cedar Rapids. I sent out a quick message to Emily letting her know that my conversation with Josh went well and thanked her for praying.

Driving to church, I felt a deep sense of gratitude to God for answering my prayers for my son and for one of the most amazing dreams I have ever had. The whole experience was surreal. I will forever be grateful!

1 Corinthians 2:9-10
However, as it is written:
"What no eye has seen,
what no ear has heard,
and what no human mind has conceived"—
the things God has prepared for those who love him—
these are the things God has revealed to us by his Spirit.
The Spirit searches all things, even the deep things of God.

eleven.

FILLED WITH HOPE

The day was finally here. The date was August 17th, 2022. *Prairie Fire Ministries* schedules their healing service every third Wednesday of the month. Emily, Josh, and I were filled with hope and anticipation for what the evening would bring as we left our home and made our way to St. Ambrose Cathedral. It took us a little over two hours to get there.

The Catholic Bishop in Des Moines, Iowa, granted permission to Graeson and his mentor and partner, Tim Jameson, to hold these monthly events in the cathedral starting in November 2021. Graeson and Tim are fueled by their love for the Lord and desire to share God's love and healing with others. This ministry took off, spreading like wildfire, and is now expanding to nearby cities and states. For those who want to learn more about it, they have a website at *https://prairiefireministries.com/*.

Emily and I attended one of the first services they held to show our support for Graeson and his newest spiritual journey. We were also curious how the evening would differ from those we had previously attended with Dr. Nemeh.

The first time we went, the event started at 7:00 p.m. and lasted several hours. We were delighted with how they orchestrated the service. We stayed until the end, uniting our prayers with those seeking healing. We didn't get back home until after midnight that night. The prayer service was unique in many ways from the ones we had previously attended with Dr. Nemeh. Each offered a beautiful, prayerful atmosphere that contributed to the healing of many who came. However, one thing remained constant - the One doing the healing was God alone.

Before we went out with Josh this time, I neglected to check if the event started at the same time, but I should have. The service had been on its way for more than an hour and a half when we arrived at 7:00 p.m. *Prairie Fire Ministries* had recently made changes to their services, starting at 5:30 p.m. instead.

The parking lot's appearance indicated that we were late. When we reached the church's front doors and saw a few people leaving,

I was crushed. I was so upset with myself for not being better prepared. As we entered the church, I made an effort to overcome my disappointment and believe that everything would be okay.

We were taken aback by the fact that despite being incredibly late, we were still greeted by a few volunteers. One of the women specifically inquired if we would be interested in signing up for the newsletter that they send out periodically. I informed her that I would be delighted. She gave me a pen, and I added my name and email to their list. Next, Josh, Emily, and I looked through the entrance of the church, searching for a seat, hoping we could sneak in without causing too much of a stir.

Josh had previously attended Dr. Nemeh's services with us but never attended a *Prairie Fire Ministries* event before. There are a few key differences in how they operate. Prayers for healing are always included in both services, and everyone present is encouraged to pray for each other. There are no variations there.

I have previously written in detail about the services we attended with Dr. Nemeh. Describing that his wife, Kathy, would usually start the event by lovingly welcoming everyone. Often, she would share recent healing stories, usually with some humorous touches. Occasionally, someone who had just been healed would be asked to talk about what happened to them. After that, Kathy introduces Dr. Nemeh. Typically, Doctor starts off by giving a short talk about spiritual matters, most often stressing the significance of the times we are currently living in.

After Dr. Nemeh has finished, the prayer service begins with volunteers calling up an average of ten people at a time to the front of the room. Those ten individuals would stand or sit in chairs while waiting for their prayer. Dr. Nemeh then proceeds to pray individually for each person, often laying his hands on those he is praying with. Instrumental Christian music softly plays in the background, creating a prayerful and reflective atmosphere, while a few volunteers stand nearby to assist anyone who may fall in the Spirit. The volunteers serve another vital purpose by being present. When Dr. Nemeh stands before someone, they quietly pray with him for that particular person.

In the same way, *Prairie Fire Ministries* begins with worship music, instructions, and stories of past healings that have occurred there. At times, they have arranged for former participants to come and talk about the healing they have received. Listening to the stories of others can help one gain spiritual strength and also create a sense of camaraderie that they are not alone in their journey.

I knew Josh was at a complete loss about what to expect because we arrived late and missed the instructions, introductions, and layout for the night. He didn't say anything, only quietly followed Emily and me into the cathedral while we searched for the best spot to sit. As we made our way forward, I noticed two distinct long lines of people waiting for their turn to confess. Having attended before, I was aware that they brought in priests from other parishes to speed up the wait times. I found it wonderful that they offered this beautiful Sacrament to help promote healing at the deepest level within one's soul.

On all sides of the altar, there were numerous prayer circles that contained the many volunteers who formed the prayer teams. In a typical team, there were at least two prayer partners who would speak with and pray for those who came up for healing.

One individual may need prayers, or several individuals, such as a whole family, would sometimes go up together. Chairs were placed in each circle to ensure that everyone could sit comfortably during their session. In total, roughly eight prayer teams were praying for various people simultaneously.

The volunteers typically consist of lay church members, including men and women of all ages. However, I have also noticed members of the clergy being involved as well. Once the service is in full swing, the Holy Spirit enters the room and fills it with God's presence. It is very comparable to what is experienced being at one of Dr. Nemeh's services.

Finally, we found a pew to sit in near the front. Before entering, we briefly bowed our heads and genuflected on both knees in our act of adoration and profound reverence as the Blessed Sacrament was exposed. After that, we scurried into the pew, pulled out the kneeler, and kneeled before the Lord one by one.

Matthew 18:19-20

"Again, truly I tell you that if two of you on earth agree about anything they ask for, it will be done for them by my Father in heaven. For where two or three gather in my name, there am I with them."

twelve.

UNPACKING THE HEART

I closed my eyes and quietly prepared my heart for what was ahead for my son. I kept reminding Jesus of what He had promised, even though I knew He hadn't forgotten. It mainly was from me attempting to have faith in what was brewing inside my heart and hoping that it would happen.

Suddenly, I felt a tapping on my shoulder. I opened my eyes to see it was coming from Josh. Leaning close, he looked around as if searching for answers, then whispered, "What is going on?"

I told him in a hushed manner how the prayer circles work. At that point, it occurred to me that he should also be aware of the lines for confession. I made a point to emphasize that most people feel the need to confess their sins before they ask God for healing. I noted that is probably why there were so many people in each line waiting for their turn. I quickly mentioned that there were many priests ministering to this Sacrament, so there shouldn't be a long wait if he wanted to go.

Motioning towards each row, I explained that they either wound back into the sacristy on one side of the church or the chapel on the other. As I pointed out each one, Josh nodded and followed my finger. However, as soon as I finished speaking, his attention returned to the beautiful display of people praying for complete strangers unfolding before us. It's clear that he was thinking that he would eventually make his own way up there. Even so, I was frustrated that he hadn't gotten in line for confession.

Soon after, Emily and I caught sight of Graeson in one of the prayer circles. We pointed him out to Josh. Graeson was aware that we were coming and why. After Josh agreed to go, I left Graeson a message explaining that God had heard our prayers for Josh. I shared with him the prophetic dream I had and how I was informed of everything that was going to happen the next day. And that it actually transpired down to the precise words, location, and time.

I informed Graeson that in my dream, I was told to bring Josh this evening and that he would be the one to pray over my son. God would then give him a miracle that would remain with him forever after that. Although it may have sounded far-fetched, I believed Graeson admired my faith in believing what was presented to me.

In my message, I thanked him for all of his recent prayers for Josh and had no doubt they played a role in what had happened so far. I informed him that we were planning to attend and asked if he could pray for my son. Graeson was overjoyed to hear that our prayers for Josh were coming to fruition, and he said he would be thrilled to help.

The service had been going on for almost two hours, and I figured Graeson had probably given up on the idea that we would even be there. As I observed him, I came to the realization that I was so absorbed in my own problems that I had forgotten the vast responsibilities he had to prepare for this healing service. His primary focus was on praying for everyone present that night. I wondered if he had even remembered that we were coming due to his incredibly busy life.

I secretly hoped that Josh would make it to the confessional as we waited to see if Graeson would notice us. When I glanced at Josh, I noticed that he was occupied entirely with watching Graeson and everyone in front of us. I returned my gaze to observe with him. Those who came for healing were gradually moving through the circles.

We observed that many were moved to tears, and others were overwhelmed with excitement over something that was felt interiorly. It was uncommon to observe someone who didn't feel anything during their prayer when watching. Even so, my own experiences have taught me that not feeling something does not imply that God did not touch that person. Healing is usually a gradual process that can occur in the days, weeks, or sometimes months ahead.

My desire for Josh to go to confession was on the rise while we waited and prayed, even though I had no idea when he last went. It became so strong that it became the only thing I could focus on. Then, I crafted up a plan of my own. My goal was to set an example.

At once, I jumped up quickly, causing Josh and Emily to raise their heads and look up at me. I whispered, "Hey, I think I am going to go get in line for confession."

Unphased by what I said, they simply just nodded their heads and went right back to monitoring how others received their prayers. Josh did not seem the least bit interested. I remained standing, feeling disappointed that I couldn't get Josh to follow my lead. I lingered for a few seconds, feeling unsure of how to proceed.

Ugh! Do I just forget it? Or should I stick to it and try to set an example? I asked myself.

Frustrated by the whole issue, I made the decision to go through with it and join the line closest to us. I stood against the wall, pouting that my plan didn't work as I had hoped. *Was anything going the way it was supposed to?* I asked myself.

I tried to unwind, switching my gaze from the floor to those receiving their prayers across the way. I noticed that Graeson was still visible from where I stood. He was moving from one prayer group to another. Since he and Tim Jameson were the ones in charge of administering this event, they also had the responsibility of overseeing all aspects of it. Likewise, they would provide extra prayers for anyone who may have needed more help or guidance during their session. I decided to pray to the Holy Spirit, asking to get Graeson's attention and that he would notice us. I kept praying, *He has to see us, Lord. He needs to know that we are here.*

Within a few minutes, Graeson hopped up from his circle and glanced around the church as if searching for someone. As I clung to the hope of what God had in store for my son, my eyes were fixed on him. At that moment, Graeson saw me, waved, and gave me a big smile. Upon noticing me, he sat back down in his circle and went straight back to praying over someone. I was amazed by the way that played out. It seemed that he had received the message from the Holy Spirit to locate me.

Knowing that Graeson was aware of our presence made me feel more confident that everything would eventually be okay. I was becoming more relaxed and started to believe that this was really going to happen. The more calm I became, the more I started to notice the music that had been playing right in front of me all along. A young man was playing the guitar while a beautiful woman quietly sang worship hymns and praised Jesus.

I began to pay more attention and let go of everything else. I was happy that we were there, and it was actually going to happen. Recognizing some of the songs, I silently mouthed the words, focusing on their meaning. Once I was fully present, the beauty of this prayerful place I was standing in brought me to tears in a matter of seconds. Despite my silent singing voice, I had faith in God's ability to hear my heart.

My mind returned to where I was standing. I was waiting in line to go to confession. *Oh Lord! What are my sins? Lord, please help me know my sins,* I pleaded.

Having knowledge of everything, God began working on my heart immediately. As I waited in line, I noticed that I had behaved poorly. God had brought us to this point; how could I doubt His plans when He had already shown me everything? We didn't HAVE to be on time. Josh didn't HAVE to go to confession for God to work in him. I was upset with myself for being so foolish.

I was a complete mess once it was time for me to enter the confessional. I entered the room, quietly closing the door behind me, stepped up to the screen, and then fell to my knees. I bowed my head and closed my eyes, hoping the priest would start quickly before I became too emotional.

When he began, my head remained lowered, and my eyes were slightly open, allowing me to make out a few things in front of me. The priest's shoes were the first thing that caught my eye. I was taken that he was wearing sandals, and not just any kind of sandals. These were flat, leather ones with straps that fastened around each foot. They were very similar to what many pictures depict Jesus wearing.

I knew going to confession is where I encounter Christ, but this striking similarity tugged at my heart and deepened my conviction to remember whom my confession was geared toward. It wasn't the priest. I came to confess my sins to Jesus.

Once my confession got underway, I realized I had become entirely fixated on things I should not have been. I had expectations of how the night should go, but nothing was going right. I was very upset with myself when we arrived late for the service. I blamed myself for Josh being unable to hear Graeson speak or get advice or tips for the night. I feared that it could affect the outcome if he didn't understand how this would all work. I was also annoyed that Josh wasn't in the confessional line with me.

I was not being a very loving person, and worst of all, I was judging my son's heart.

I started weeping, attempting to communicate through my tears all the ways I had failed just in the last hour alone. I felt completely ashamed of myself.

The priest quietly listened to my rant. He informed me that my troubles were not complicated. He outlined every issue, giving advice for each one. He told me that being late didn't matter in the least. "God sees him there and knows why he came," Father told me.

He spoke about the ways my son encounters Christ, which is why I wanted him to go to confession in the first place. Then he said, "Your son has been encountering Christ every time he is around you. And he knows it."

I was deeply moved by that statement. He recommended that I turn my troubles over to God and let Him handle everything for me.

I immediately stopped crying. Through the words of the priest, I felt peace in my heart. I expressed my gratitude to him for his kindness and wisdom and for putting me back in my proper place. As I left, I snuck one last peek at those sandals that reminded me of Jesus' presence in that room. The moment I left the confessional, I felt refreshed and filled with the love of Jesus. Moreover, it gave me the assurance that my heart would remain content even if the evening didn't go completely as planned.

Psalm 32:5

Then I acknowledged my sin to you
and did not cover up my iniquity.
I said, "I will confess
my transgressions to the Lord."
And you forgave
the guilt of my sin.

thirteen.

DEEP IN THE DIRT

During my absence, Josh and Emily had not moved an inch. I kneeled beside them and completed the prayers I was instructed to say for my penance. As soon as I was done, I raised my head and looked around the church, wondering where Graeson had gone. After a few minutes, I found him. He was praying in yet another circle. I was eager to talk to Graeson about what we needed to do. So again, I invoked my prayers to the Holy Spirit, requesting that Graeson be directed to come our way soon.

In less than a minute, Graeson sprung up from his chair and made a beeline for us, smiling all the way. Once he reached our pew, Graeson gave Emily and me a warm welcome hug, *'hello.'*

Graeson turned his attention to Josh and offered to shake his hand.

"It's great to finally meet you, Josh," Graeson said, continuing with his friendly greeting.

Suddenly my excitement kicked in, and without much consideration, I blurted, "Graeson, can you please pray for Josh?"

I immediately recognized how ridiculous that sounded, particularly because Graeson had just introduced himself and even more so because many people were still waiting for their prayers. To save face, I offered another proposal, "Well, I mean, perhaps it would be better to wait until after the service is over, especially since we were so late?"

Although I was aware that Graeson could hear my babbling, he remained entirely focused on my son. Graeson pondered the more significant issue at hand, asking, "Josh, would you like to receive a prayer?"

Guardedly, Josh replied, "Yes."

Graeson was delighted by the answer and gave a reassuring smile. He placed one hand on Josh's left shoulder and said, "Alright, there's a line over there for those who are waiting for prayers." He motioned across the aisle towards a small group of people sitting in chairs placed ahead of all the pews.

"You can have a seat over there and wait for when it's your turn to come up," he continued.

Graeson made it clear that he was a "floater." He promised that whichever prayer team Josh was directed to, he would make sure to come over and pray for him.

Emily, Josh, and I headed to the waiting area while Graeson continued to pray with others and move from one team to another. The Holy Spirit was clearly guiding his every move. I was slightly nervous that Graeson wouldn't notice Josh when he went up there. I envisioned future scenarios in my mind. I quickly became concerned that Graeson might encounter a serious situation that could prevent him from leaving a prayer circle and joining Josh's. I was trying to trust, but honestly, I was finding it hard to stay positive because I knew what was at stake.

As we watched one person go up after another, we slid down the line accordingly. After us, several others came over to the area and took their seats. As I looked around, I realized that there were still a few people in the church who seemed to be praying for the courage to get in line. In my mind, it seemed that either everyone had already been prayed for or they were seated ahead of us. Once again, my assumptions were completely off.

At last, our time had come. This was it! Despite being next in line, I was uncertain about the circle we would be sent to. The three of us were anxiously watching to see where Josh would end up. Josh became more and more uneasy as the minutes went by. At some point, he started to fidget, bounce his legs, and take a few deep breaths. I was also anxious, praying that Graeson wouldn't miss him when it was his turn.

Lo and behold, a circle opened up. It was the very one that Graeson was sitting in at the time. Upon the completion of praying for the two individuals, they all stood up and hugged each other. I watched as Graeson scouted the area for the next person. A radiant smile encircled his face once he noticed that it was Josh. I was elated! It couldn't have worked out any more perfectly than it did.

Emily leaned in and inquired if Josh wanted us to join him for his prayer session. Josh responded casually, "Sure." Mentioning that he could benefit from all the additional prayers.

We stood up together and walked up the steps to meet Graeson and the prayer team. There were three other volunteers in this group, all women, who were there to pray for Josh as well. One of the volunteers grabbed another chair to ensure there were enough seats for everyone.

Graeson greeted Josh as we approached and shook his hand again. I glanced over to the three young women, who were sitting in their seats and appeared to be praying for Josh already.

The four of us, Josh, Graeson, Emily, and I, remained standing in a circle of our own when Graeson addressed Josh with some concern. "Josh, are you sure you want your mom and sister up here with you?"

Josh shrugged, claiming, "I mean, yeah, that's fine."

It was apparent to me that Graeson did not think it was a wise idea. He gently cautioned Josh, "Where weeds are growing, if you just cut them off at the base, they will grow back."

"We must go deep in the dirt and cast all of it out."

Josh seemed unsure of what to do or say. Then Graeson went about trying to make his point another way. Graeson spoke to Josh about his purity because he is fully aware of the love and goodness of God. Our God, who looks past our sins and surrounds us with His grace and goodness. He communicated that the evil one does just the opposite, trying to use what is the truest sense about a person against them.

At last, Josh comprehended what Graeson was alluding to and heeded his advice. Turning to Emily and me, Josh mildly announced, "Okay, yeah, sorry. It is probably better if I go alone."

Emily and I both agreed and returned to our seats. Our attention was solely focused on observing what was going to happen next. Graeson was the one leading the prayers in the group. He was asking Josh some questions, and Josh was responding. It wasn't long before I noticed my son was in the Spirit. His head was tilted slightly back and swaying gently back and forth. Emily and I exchanged glances several times with tears in our eyes. We had been praying and hoping for this moment for a long time.

It came to my attention that Graeson was asking Josh to repeat certain words to him, but I couldn't make out what they were. Graeson would speak and occasionally tap on Josh's chest, right where his heart was as if he was attempting to open up his hardened heart.

They spoke back and forth, alternately, until suddenly, the momentum stopped. It was clear to me that something was wrong. It became evident that they had reached a matter that was extremely hard for Josh to let go of. His eyes fluttered open, and he turned away, gazing at the ground. Josh shook his head.

Somehow, in that moment, I was able to read Josh's lips when he spoke the two words, "I can't."

I didn't know what to make of this roadblock. I felt a sudden surge of nervousness come over me. I don't think I was blinking or breathing. As far as I know, my heart may have stopped beating too. I am not sure.

Emily and I exchanged looks again, this time because of our fear of missing out on the promised miracle. As we continued watching, we prayed harder for Josh. Graeson didn't let up either. He continued to pursue Josh with full strength. Graeson's face was filled with determination as he intensified his prayers. He was literally praying over Josh's heart over and over, saying one prayer after another, and then tapping on his heart each time.

"Come on, Josh," I prayed with each tap Graeson performed.

After a few minutes of this incredible and powerful display of Graeson's fortitude, and unwillingness to give in, Josh did it! His heart finally opened, and the tears instantly spilled out. Josh's entire body and posture appeared to be liberated. The same relief was reflected in his countenance as well. As he spoke with Graeson about his struggles, he was wiping away many tears.

Shortly after, Graeson moved Josh to the Blessed Sacrament that was displayed in the Monstrance on top of the Altar. Graeson placed his hand firmly on Josh's back, asking him to kneel next to him and be present face-to-Face, eye-to-Eye, and heart-to-Heart with our Lord. Graeson stayed with him, praying while they remained in the same position for some time.

I caught sight of Emily out of the corner of my eye at this point. She was discreetly holding up her phone and snapping a quick photo before quickly putting it back in her pocket. She gave me a sweet smile and whispered, "I just knew I was supposed to do that...to capture this special moment."

2 Corinthians: 5:17

Therefore, if anyone is in Christ, the new creation has come: The old has gone, the new is here!

fourteen.

A HEART OF FLESH

The moment Josh surrendered that night was incredibly moving for Emily and me. I am not sure which one of us was more emotional. We heard another person sniffling around the same time as if they were crying, too, coming from behind us. We both turned around to see what was wrong and were surprised to see two familiar and friendly faces smiling back at us.

It was our dear friends Butch and Mary Lou Milling. Mary Lou was the one who was shedding tears. This beautiful couple has been with us many times to Ohio for Dr. Nemeh's prayer services. They had come this same night seeking prayers of their own. After realizing we were there and what was happening, they stayed a bit longer to participate in praying for Josh, too. I couldn't believe it. They did not attend this service in Des Moines frequently, especially since it was two hours away from their home. I credited God for arranging a special moment to be shared with two of our closest friends.

The service was nearly over by the time Graeson finished praying with Josh. The gentleman who played the guitar earlier was now also singing. The music grew in intensity after all of the prayer teams were done. Before I knew it, we were immersed in a sea of beautiful voices praising God's great love and mercy. I had to sing along with the crowd because the joy I felt couldn't be contained.

The remnant that remained after the prayers were finished that evening did not solely worship God with their voice. Some were on their faces, others on their knees, and the remaining individuals stood, most of whom had their arms raised high. The display of love for God was overwhelming! Josh, Emily, and I stood shoulder-to-shoulder, wiping away tears as we praised our Lord. At that moment, Josh turned towards me, lifted me slightly from the ground, and gave me a strong bear hug, whispering in my ear, "Thank you, Mom!"

I was reminded of the mixed emotions experienced by nearly everyone who attended our bus pilgrimages years ago when I drove home that night. People were feeling anxious and unsure of what to expect on the way to Ohio, but everyone was cheerful and full of the Holy Spirit on the way back.

This trip felt very much the same way. For miles and miles, we drove home feeling refreshed, relieved from the heaviness we each carried to Des Moines. The joy of the Lord filled the car on our way home. It was unmistakable, even palpable.

Josh and Emily were conversing about how they would describe everything that took place if they were talking to someone about the night. They were both in agreement. There were no words. It was impossible for anyone to adequately express what was felt. It was totally "Indescribable," they laughed joyously.

These two kept repeating that same phrase over and over again. After a while they burst into laughter about just how indescribable it really was for all of us. Emily playfully offered to write a book about the night, titling it *Indescribable,* but warned that the inside of the book would have to be left completely blank. All of us quieted down, seemingly pondering what she had just said. Emily may have thought we didn't understand the joke because then she made herself even more clear by stating, "There would be no words inside it, because, well, it is just indescribable!"

After this comical clarification, those two were laughing so hard they could hardly speak.

I noticed how Josh appeared to be a different person now. I had not seen him smile like that or heard him laugh so hard in such a long time. I was grateful for Josh's willingness to trust what I shared with him the week before about plans I believed God had for him. He could have easily dismissed everything I told him and just ignored the healing service option like nothing. But he didn't. Josh trusted everything I said, and most importantly, he believed that God had the ability to renew his spirit.

I don't think Josh has any idea how much watching him exercise his faith like that has impacted and strengthened my own faith in return. Observing him through the dashboard lights, I saw a beautiful light coming from his eyes when he turned to look at me. In my heart, I just know that what I saw was the Light of Christ shining through them, just like it used to before his troubles set in.

I never asked Josh about the issues, which he would later describe as his 'darkest hour'. All I knew was that he seemed powerless to overcome the situation without bringing God into the equation.

About an hour into our drive, the ride became very quiet. All of us, no doubt, were replaying the entire evening in our minds. Josh was staring out into the night sky when he acknowledged, "Jesus delivered me from a lot tonight."

Later, Josh broke through the stillness again, stating his gratitude for Graeson and all the ways that he helped him pull through. He expressed his desire to return to the healing service next month to personally thank Graeson for all of his prayers.

I spoke with Graeson myself a few days later. I couldn't express my gratitude in any other way than by telling him that this night was one of the top five in my entire life!

A few days after that special event, while attending daily Mass, I noticed my son walking through the church doors. He smiled, waved, and then proceeded to enter the confession line.

I was immediately brought back to the healing service and the foolish thoughts I had that night. Here, I stood corrected in my religious ideologies. Sometimes, there are certain steps that should be taken to find healing, but I have also seen times when God intervenes differently. God's ways are not our ways, and we cannot limit what God can do based on our actions. We cannot earn forgiveness or love. Being able to receive it openly is a grace.

Therefore, God did not need my son to go to confession first in order to reach him. The only requirement was for Josh to be searching for Him. When we are ready, God, the Good Father, will come run to meet us, even if we don't have ourselves cleaned up spiritually first. Grace is the means by which we receive, and the healing and changes it brings to our lives are meant to glorify God all the more.

Josh came over and sat beside me after making his way through the confessional. After Mass, we went outside to talk before going our separate ways. We noticed our good friend Butch as he was driving away and acknowledged him with a wave '*hello*.'

As soon as Butch saw us, he promptly turned his pickup around, parked it, and hiked over to speak with us. More specifically, to talk to Josh.

Butch came over, hugged us, and then curiously glanced at Josh and asked, "You had a healing last week, didn't you?"

Josh's face lit up with a bright and happy smile.

Butch beamed back a smile of his own. With excitement coming through his voice, he declared, "I could see it when you were in front of the Altar looking at the Blessed Sacrament."

About that time, Sue Manternach, a good friend of mine and Butch's, saw us standing on the street corner. She, too, was departing from church and heading towards her parked car. She hesitantly approached us, gleaming ever so cutely, asking if we were okay with her joining our conversation.

"By all means! Come over and join us," I chirped.

Briefly, I introduced the two of them, "Sue, this is my son, Josh."

Josh extended his hand, offering, "Hi, I am Joshua."

I did a double take. "*Joshua?*"

I had not heard him use that name since he was a young child. While staring at him, Sue interrupted my thoughts and asked, "Are you guys discussing miracles?"

I was unsure of how she knew that, but we confirmed that "yes," we certainly were, and that Josh had a BIG miracle happen in his heart.

Sue misunderstood what I meant by that, bidding, "Oh. Wow. What was going on with your heart, Joshua?"

I couldn't help laughing because, by her question, I realized that I didn't clarify that very well, "No, no. I am so sorry. I meant to say that God gave him a new heart. A heart of flesh."

Still uncertain by what I meant, Sue glanced back towards Josh with a concerned look, "Oh, but what was wrong with your heart?"

"Nothing was wrong with it." Josh was now beaming and added, "God changed me and brought me back to Him."

We stood discussing the matter on that street corner for at least thirty minutes when Josh had to leave and head back to work.

Then Sue addressed what I noticed during the car ride home that one exceptional evening, "Christy! Your son's eyes! They were SO bright. They were almost glowing!"

As I walked back to my car, I thought about how Josh introduced himself. To me, that seemed so peculiar. Once I got inside, I removed my phone and turned back on the ringer. I noticed that I had received a voicemail from Graeson while in church. As I listened to it, I was given the answer to my wonderings.

Graeson informed me that while praying for my son, he began to address him as Joshua. Graeson said it was only fitting for him to do so, as God was changing everything about him that night. When God does that, He often gives us a new name, like Simon being called Peter and Saul of Tarsus being under the new name of Paul. Graeson mentioned when he called Josh Joshua, his eyes seemed to light right up in front of him.

In my journal that day, I wrote, "I am incredibly grateful for everything God has done for *Joshua*. He is so different. It appears that God has taken away his troubles, reshaped him, and aided him in remembering this with the new name of Joshua."

Joshua was his God-given birth name. The meaning of Joshua's name is 'The Lord Is Salvation' and 'Yahweh Saves'.

Ezekiel 36:26

I will give you a new heart and put a new spirit in you; I will remove from you your heart of stone and give you a heart of flesh.

fifteen.

CHILDLIKE FAITH

In the past few years, I have come to understand that God is intimately involved in the details of our lives, frequently orchestrating things behind the scenes. Nothing is insignificant to Him. Oftentimes, we are unaware of the reason He leads us to certain things or specific people until a later, more opportune time. God determines when and how we will see the effects of what He has called us to do. All we need are ears to hear and a willingness to obey, even if things may seem random at the time. Trusting that He has a greater purpose in mind for every situation.

I have been made aware of this reality multiple times. Toward the end of 2022, I was once again shown how He works through our circumstances in marvelous ways. The same month Joshua underwent his incredible transformation, Emily began her first official teaching role at a local elementary school. I proposed that I could come to the classroom and assist with the children's writing and reading skills on occasion.

Emily immediately accepted my offer. She asked me one day if I would be interested in reading a book to the class.

I considered the question, echoing, "Read to the class?"

I'm not a person who enjoys being in front of a group. However, I would have never guessed that the thought of being in front of a class of fifth graders would cause me to feel nervous, but it did.

"Uh, sure! What would you like me to read?" I asked, under the impression that it would be a short novel, making it a one-time event.

Emily replied, "Your first book."

It's probable that in that instant, my eyes grew to the size of saucers. "My first book?!" I repeated her words, perplexed by her reply. My tone was clearly conveying the astonishment I felt.

"Yes, your first book. I just know it is something that you should do."

"What? Why? Fifth graders would never be interested in listening to me read a two-hundred-and-something-page book," I nervously said with a bit of a chuckle.

"Plus, I am not sure I should be reading about miracles and the like to young children," I added.

"What are you talking about, Mom? The local Catholic bookstore is selling your book, and children need to hear about miracles. It's important for them to understand that this spiritual world exists and that it is real."

"You don't have to read it all at once. Just like one chapter, maybe, a few times a week," Emily reassured me.

I agreed to try it out, but I was seriously pondering whether it was a good idea or if the kids would like it. The first day I arrived to do so, I was shocked at the level of interest across the room. Emily had already shared some parts of her miracle stories with the class and about Dr. Nemeh with them. It seemed like they were eager to learn more.

I would come in to continue reading the story based on how our calendars aligned. There was no predetermined schedule, and the frequency of my visits varied each week. Sometimes, it was every day, and other times, only once a week. Admittedly, there were days when the class genuinely seemed to show more interest than others. Regardless of the day or chapter, there were always a couple of kids who were completely captivated by what I was reading. These few seemed connected to every word I read, sometimes even showing emotion. The fact that young kids seemed drawn to it, especially at that level, was both surprising and impressive to me.

After months of reading the book to the class, I finally finished it when Emily was approached by one of her students after school. The child had a family friend currently suffering from stage IV cancer and wondered if Dr. Nemeh could pray for him. My daughter's heart was greatly touched by this child's faith.

I wrote a lengthy letter to this student's parents after Emily shared this information with me. I slipped this letter inside one of the extra copies of the book I had lying around and handed it to Emily. I requested that she send it back with the student to give it to her parents. I wanted to make it clear that the stories in the book I was reading were entirely genuine and not fabricated. The book was a true reflection of the miracles that happened to us and the people chronicled in it.

The mother sent an email to my daughter, her child's teacher, thanking us for reaching out. She was now reading the book on her own and was amazed by our experiences. Through her understanding of how God works in our lives every day, she realized that people are often placed in our lives for a purpose. In regard to this friend that her child was worried about, she told us he was a truly wonderful man. She found him to be quite open to the idea of receiving prayers from Dr. Nemeh after talking to him about what had happened to us.

They immediately signed this man up for a virtual prayer call with Dr. Nemeh. And, as we have seen many times before, God miraculously opened a spot for him in no time at all. In her email, she requested that we keep this man in our prayers for the weekend of his appointment. She mentioned that she had kept spreading the message by giving the book to others who she thought would benefit and enjoy reading it.

After returning to school on Monday, the student spoke with my daughter, Miss Blake, about the event. The family friend arranged for the mom and daughter to attend his prayer session with him, particularly since he had learned about Dr. Nemeh from them. When describing the virtual prayer, the student said it was a wonderful experience to be a part of. She observed that the man frequently mentioned experiencing physical sensations within his body.

We would have to wait to see what his prayer session would bring about in the days ahead. No matter the results, it was clear to everyone that this child's faith and trust in what God could do played a crucial role in making this happen for him.

Mark 10:14-15

He said to them, "Let the little children come to me, and do not hinder them, for the kingdom of God belongs to such as these. Truly I tell you, anyone who will not receive the kingdom of God like a little child will never enter it."

sixteen.

GIFTS MEANT TO BE SHARED

Around this same time, I had to pay a visit to my own physician for what would be my last time. I had been trying to renew my migraine medicines through our mail-order pharmacy for weeks without any success. Migraines are the one thing I have been unable to get rid of completely. But despite the suffering I have now and then with a migraine, it is nothing compared to how awful and sick I felt before 2019. Given what Jesus has taken away from me, I have no room to complain.

Despite my repeated attempts to order a refill, the receptionist called me to tell me that my physician had declined the request, insisting that I visit the office first. I couldn't for the life of me understand why she refused. It was common for her to renew the medication without me having to call. Normally, our online pharmacy handled everything electronically. I was a bit perplexed and honestly felt a little annoyed.

I was not using my spiritual perspective when I passed through the front door of the medical clinic in mid-November 2022. I was solely focused on myself and didn't consider the impact that my appointment could later have on her life. Receiving my medication was my primary concern at the time.

The staff checked me in, transferred me to a room, and reviewed all the standard questions. After the nurse left, I sat in the patient's chair and waited for my physician. I was thinking about the many tasks I had to do that day, hoping things would speed up once I saw my doctor. After a long wait, she finally entered the room and offered me one of her sweet and warm smiles. She expressed her deep regret for the extended delay *and* for asking that I come into the office.

The latter part of her apology still confused me, *Why was I here?* I contemplated.

Oh well, I thought, taking in a deep, cleansing breath and shrugging off my frustrations.

At last, I made the decision to let it go and make the most of my presence. Plus, my physician truly was the best and I valued having her as my doctor. She deserved my patience and kindness. The main reason I was frustrated was my busy schedule. Also, I was still confused why she refused to renew my prescription to begin with.

"No worries. It is nice to see you again," I expressed.

We hadn't seen each other in nearly two years. Two years ago, my doctor attended the big virtual healing service that Emily and I helped organize, bringing hundreds of people together for prayers with Dr. Nemeh. She was present with her parents and even contributed to the event by suggesting ways to make people feel safe during the early stages of COVID.

I was watching her closely. She seemed emotional while clicking and looking through my information on her laptop. She abruptly stopped what she was doing and closed the computer. As she sat perfectly still and gazed down, she seemed to be lost in her thoughts. I knew then that something was not right. She turned her body towards me on the swivel chair and stared at me motionlessly for a long, silent minute before speaking.

Again, apologizing for having me come in, she related, "But I had to decline the refill so that I could get you to come into the office."

Once more, I was not following. I needed more context. Tears were now visible in her eyes as she continued, "I am closing my practice and taking some time off."

I waited for more information as I shook my head in disbelief. My physician mentioned that she's had a lot of heart issues since she was a child, including heart surgery. Recently, things had taken a turn for the worse, and she was passing out on occasion. Her doctors all agreed that it was most likely caused by the same heart issue that had plagued her most of her life.

In recent months, she had been subjected to much testing and was often wearing a Holter Monitor. Her condition was worsening, and she was dealing with anxiety as a new symptom. She was worried about what would happen next. Although she didn't want to do this, she believed she had no other choice.

It was a sad moment for me to have to say goodbye to my physician. She was a woman of strong faith. She mentioned that most patients received a letter in the mail. Due to our recent bonding over my healing and stories of others who were touched by God, she desired to speak with me in person about the situation.

After giving me the sad news, she began to ask more questions about Dr. Nemeh and inquired if I could share more details about recent events. We had a lengthy conversation about the miracles I had witnessed in the past two years, and the books I had written that included some of them. She was extremely receptive and had complete faith in everything I spoke about. Even though she was having to close her practice due to her own health problems, she was the one relishing in the miracle stories of others.

She let me know after a while that she had another thing she wanted to discuss with me.

I sat up straight in my chair, curious about what she was referring to, asking, "Oh yeah?"

Leaning in, she quickly reassured me that it was all good news this time. She served as a board member on the committee for the annual women's conference in her local parish. They were searching for a speaker, so she recently suggested my name as a possible candidate. She testified to the committee about my healing, having personally witnessed it during my time under her care. She encouraged me with her kind smile and inquired if I was willing to discuss the disease I had endured for so long. She intended for me to share with others about my healing and the many ways God had transformed me through it.

I was overcome with surprise. I had no idea what to say. In truth, the mere thought of speaking in front of a group ignited a fear in me. I pushed through the overwhelming immediate reaction and informed my physician that I would do it if they selected me. If God was asking this of me, there was no way I could refuse Him, especially after everything He has done for me.

As I walked out to my car that morning, I felt remorseful for how I had approached my appointment when I entered. I was still in a state of confusion after hearing all the news she had just shared. As soon as I entered my car, I sent a message to my husband regarding the nature of my visit. He was also curious about why I had to go in instead of them refilling my medication as usual. After sending that text, I was about to leave the parking lot when I felt a sudden nudge to give my doctor a copy of both books. The same books that contained many of the stories we were reminiscing about for almost an hour. It was clear to me that God was asking me to do this.

I found a small piece of paper and wrote her a short note that I was giving them as a gift, with no expectation of anything in return. After shutting off my engine, I removed the two books from the trunk and marched back inside. I gave them to the receptionist, requesting that she give them to my doctor. Despite her curious nodding, she still gave a warm smile. I left the office feeling a mixture of emotions.

Luckily for me, and perhaps also for that group of women, I learned later that the committee had chosen someone else who was probably more suitable for the role. Although I was relieved to say it mildly, I am certain that God knows that if He had chosen me to do it, I would have done so.

I remained in contact with my physician through Facebook Messenger. One day, she unexpectedly asked if we were planning to travel to Ohio any time soon. I replied, "Yes, as a matter of fact, I am going (for me) to see Dr. Nemeh in late December (2022)."

I mentioned that I suffered a disc injury in my back from snow shoveling and experienced minor sleep disturbances while also still suffering from those pesky migraines. I wrote, "I am not sure if there is a limit on how many miracles a person can ask for."

We exchanged messages for a brief period. Then, I inquired, "Do you have any prayer requests? I am writing some up for him (Dr. Nemeh) to pray over after my time with him. I would love to add anything you would like."

She submitted several petitions for her parents and one for her own recent health concerns. I informed her to keep the intentions in her heart on the day of my appointment. She thanked me and asked me to keep her informed of how things went.

During my stay in Ohio, my doctor sent me another message. Coincidentally, the very same morning I was there for my appointment with Dr. Nemeh, a friend of hers had reached out to her. The friend was asking questions specifically about me and my first book and reported that she had heard about my story.

Then she had some more inquiries concerning Emily. This friend was trying to determine if Emily and her son's teacher were the same person. My physician didn't know the answer, so she relayed the question to me. I responded, "Yes. That is her. Emily currently teaches fifth grade there. Why?"

The boy had informed his mother that I would come and read my book to the class. He wasn't the same child that I mentioned earlier with the family friend, this was a different student.

My physician said, "He's been recounting the miracle stories to his mom. And, well, now this kid's grandmother has also learned about them and is now very interested in visiting Ohio."

I considered how incredible it was that despite giving a small portion of my day to reading to these children, it still made a significant impact on several individuals. It all came down to Emily following through with the nudge she had and asking me to do it. The fact that it affected the families and friends of these children was truly inspirational and something I couldn't have predicted on my own.

I learned more about my doctor's condition through our communication in the days ahead. Near the area where she had previous surgeries, her doctors had recently discovered a small hole in her heart. She informed me in a later message that she had signed up for a virtual prayer session with Dr. Nemeh. She was also hoping to attend one of the upcoming monthly Zoom meetings.

During the monthly Zoom meeting in April 2023, I spotted that my physician was on the call with us, along with almost one hundred others. As we listened and watched, her name appeared in the group chat. I leaned in to see what she wrote. I was astonished when reading her words, which stated she had experienced a beautiful miracle!

She wrote that she had a private prayer session with Dr. Nemeh and now fully believes in what God can do. Although she witnessed God's work through me, it's a much different story when it is your own body. The hole that had been detected through medical imaging and documented by other doctors was no longer there. God healed her through the power of a prayer, just like He did me and countless others who have gone to Dr. Nemeh.

I had no idea how her prayer session had gone until that moment. I was so excited for her that I wanted to jump up and down for joy!

It was later revealed to Emily and me that the friend of the family who was prayed over via Zoom also experienced a miracle during his prayer session. Shortly afterwards, he learned that his stage IV cancer was no longer detectable. It was gone!

Our own testimonies are important to speak to others about, just like the stories in the Gospels are composed mainly of individual witnesses. They are gifts meant to be shared! It's often difficult to observe the impact it has on individuals, but it almost always ends up reaching those who need to hear it the most. The Holy Spirit takes action when it reaches them, letting them know that God is with them and can heal them. In bearing our witness, one thing is for sure - no one can predict how far it will travel or who it will meet.

Isaiah 55:11
so is my word that goes out from my mouth:
It will not return to me empty,
but will accomplish what I desire
and achieve the purpose for which I sent it.

seventeen.

LIVING THE DREAM...IN SPANISH

I already wrote about my difficulties in falling away from following the Lord at the beginning of 2023. After fighting back with my faith in the healing that God had given me and renouncing Satan, I was able to bounce right back. Diligently, I went back to praying and blessing the Lord with my heart and life again.

Immediately after, I received numerous signs that I was once again on the right path. One of them was that we would be bringing two more individuals to see Dr. Nemeh. In addition to everything else, I carried out other plans that I believed the Lord was asking of me, like making the second book available in audio format. To accomplish this, I recorded small audio segments every morning in a small closet in our basement.

God began providing me with ways to follow the path He had for me after making a better effort to live the way I should. One of the ways He communicated with me was to give me dreams about various ideas. More often than not, they seemed impossible, sometimes almost laughable. One of which occurred while I was still recording audio for the second book. I was shown that I should translate my first book into another language. I had a dream where I saw Spanish-speaking communities, Hispanic churches, and even people I knew as a child who were Hispanic. I observed that every person was reading a book. I became aware that the book they were reading was my first and that it was written in their native language. When I woke up, I was apprehensive about what I felt He was asking me to do.

I questioned my interpretation of the dream. *Lord, you know that I am not qualified for this, don't you? My Spanish vocabulary is limited to only a few words.*

He persevered in clarifying His will, especially since I was uncertain if the dream was really what He was asking of me. One day, someone unexpectedly asked me if I had ever considered translating my book into Spanish. Ding. Ding. Ding. I realized that He was truly asking me to do this, and the dream was not just any ordinary one. I was thankful for His persistence in fully revealing His plans.

Eventually, I asked around to see if anyone had any insight into how I could get this done. I began by asking acquaintances who attended the Spanish-speaking Mass at our church. After that didn't work, I tried asking another friend whom I met revolving around Dr. Nemeh's prayers who resides in California. Each time, my requests were unsuccessful. Even though these individuals tried to help, my efforts failed to yield any results. Until one day, I asked my dear friend Hallina.

Hallina got in touch with me a while ago when she was reading my first book and going to see Dr. Nemeh for the first time. She said that when traveling from her hometown in Massachusetts to Westlake, Ohio, she listened to a recorded version of my first book to help her overcome the obstacles with traveling. She gained confidence and hope for what God had in store for her by hearing me read the accounts of Jesus walking into my life and healing many. Listening to it, she was able to feel God's loving protection, allowing her to move past the anxiety and fear that were holding her back.

Hallina's description of how my first book helped her overcome her uncertainties touched me deeply. Halina's words motivated me to carry on with my mission of writing and sharing more stories about Jesus' healing of many people.

From the moment we first spoke, I knew that God had placed us in each other's lives for a great purpose. Each time we communicated, I felt a strong connection to her. We have been friends for some time now. Our usual discussions tend to revolve around spiritual matters such as our love for Jesus, our faith, the beauty and trials of life, and our love for the Nemehs.

From the beginning, I noticed that despite life's hardships, Hallina remains extremely positive while always displaying a deep, strong faith and love for the Lord. Over time, our friendship has grown. Frequently, we reach out to each other to say hello, ask for prayers when necessary, or just to check in to let the other know we are thinking about them.

When I was struggling with fulfilling God's request, I asked Hallina if she had any contacts who could assist me in translating my book. She didn't. But boy, did she take my request seriously. She got back to me in a matter of days and gave me the name of someone who could be of assistance. She came across an individual who specialized in such matters on the Fiverr app. Hallina not only found someone, but she also made sure to find someone who was both good and affordable.

In no time at all, God directed Hallina to the perfect platform and professional freelancer to do the job, even though I had been searching full-time for weeks. I wanted to repay her for her kindness and time. But she wouldn't hear of it, saying that the most important thing was to make sure the book was accessible to those who needed it translated. Hallina was a true angel.

It never failed. Through dreams or by other means, God would direct me to what He desired. What is more, whenever I doubted my abilities or if I was truthfully hearing from Him, He would use someone or a situation to help guide me the right way. When we search for Him, He will reveal the path and open doors.

Psalm 16:7

I will praise the Lord, who counsels me;
even at night my heart instructs me.

eighteen.

THE BIG SQUEEZE

I had come such a long way in just a few months. I transitioned from feeling sorry for myself, being spiritually lazy, and physically sick, to once again praying, surrendering to His daily will, and doing good works for Him. Kathy Nemeh's approach of "praying your way through each and every day" was the only way I could achieve this.

While I was almost done recording book two, my first book was in the process of being translated. During this same time, my friend, Sue Manternach was feeling called by the Holy Spirit to start up a faith-based organization in the Cedar Rapids, Iowa area.

Sue believed that God was leading her to establish a platform that would provide multiple ways for individuals to volunteer in the community based on the Corporal Works of Mercy.

She reached out to me and my daughter Emily for assistance. The three of us worked together to create a website that showcased organizations in our area that aligned with our beliefs and provided ways for people to serve. This inspired idea came shortly after she found her own set of miracles from an appointment with Dr. Nemeh. I included her miracle story in my second book, *The Power of God... Tomorrow.*

Emily and I were both humbled and honored to help Sue do this for our community. We hoped that it would be a valuable resource for many, enriching one's faith and maybe even aiding in the discovery of their charisms in the process. The fact that we were called to work together to make this a reality was a blessing for all of us. We created an organization called *Mission of Mercy Magnified* that allows people to browse through and find the most effective ways to volunteer. Our website can be viewed by visiting: *missionofmercymagnified.org*.

I was occupied with multiple projects simultaneously, reducing my time for anything else on the side. However, the idea that I discussed with my accountant months ago kept coming to mind. I strongly felt compelled to transform *The Blessed Reason Trip* into a charity.

I was uncertain about these feelings and was curious why they kept coming. *Perhaps I was dreaming up this idea all on my own?* I wondered.

I was constantly praying for guidance because this feeling was not going away. One day in early March, after going up and receiving Holy Communion at Mass, God intervened to help me know what to do. A beautiful vision was given to me while I was kneeling and praying. In it, Jesus appeared wearing a red robe, standing behind me, and extending His right hand over me. I was immediately aware that this gesture signified His blessing for me to move forward with what continued to come to my mind.

I kept my head bowed, praying. I was completely taken aback by what I observed.

However, once more, I was questioning if this was just my imagination tricking me, especially when I was desperately searching for an answer.

Lord, how do I know this is really from you? How can I know that I truly just witnessed Your presence, and this was not a figment of my imagination?

No answer was given.

I started tearing up due to my uncertainty....and my unbelief.

Praying with all my heart, I silently cried, *Lord, Please...PLEASE give me a PHYSICAL sign that this is you.*

Right then and there, a big squeeze was given to my right arm. I jumped and nearly screamed when it happened. That physical sign had only taken a matter of seconds to manifest. I was not expecting anything like that to happen, especially at that exact moment.

I raised my head and tried to see who had squeezed my arm through my teary eyes. There was no one there. I trembled in confusion. As soon as I turned around to see who it might have been, I saw a woman. She wore an all-white, long, flowing dress and a wide-brimmed hat. Her back was turned to me as she made her way down the aisle behind me.

Despite being in total shock, I continued watching. At some point, the woman turned around to look back at me. After giving me a warm smile, she strolled into a pew across the church. It was challenging for me to comprehend everything that had just occurred.

Struggling to make sense of it all, I could hardly move. *Who was that? Was she an angel in disguise?*

I reverted to my kneeling position, facing the right direction, and sunk down to the ground, resting my head on the pew before me. I was hesitant to look at her again, but eventually, I managed to do so and realized that I was actually familiar with this woman.

Her name is Lisa DeWees. I had met her previously, but it had been several years ago. We arranged a time to talk about Dr.

Nemeh and the many miracles surrounding him. When we originally met, she struck me as someone with a profoundly deep faith. She spoke with great love and admiration about her family, friends, and the community as a whole during our conversation. Meeting her was a joy, and I knew she would be someone I would always remember.

As I continued to kneel, I heard Father request that everyone stand for the final blessing. I was still a bit shaken, trying to calm down my nerves. Later, as I left church and walked to my car, I came to the realization that my reaction probably frightened her. In fact, it was possible that I had scared her a lot.

On my drive home, I kept replaying what happened over and over again in my mind. The vision of Jesus blessing our organization to become a charity. The "physical" sign I requested was delivered by God in a real physical form. The timing of Lisa's squeeze and how she was dressed that day were incredible. She literally looked like an angel to me.

I chuckled to myself, She *WAS my angel.*

Angels are God's Heavenly messengers, and God surely just used Lisa to convey the message that everything I experienced was genuine.

When I got home, I texted Lisa to apologize for any fear I may have caused her when she was just trying to say "hello."

I wrote:

Hi Lisa, was it you that stopped by after communion today? If so, I apologize for my deer-in-the-headlights look. Lol. I was deep in prayer, and the timing of that arm squeeze was quite amazing! I had just asked God to please provide me with a physical sign affirming His blessing on starting a nonprofit that I have felt Him asking me to start, and about a second or two later, you did that. I almost jumped out of my skin! Lol, and then, of course, it took my mind a few seconds to figure out who you were because, at first glance, I thought you were an angel.

I have a feeling that my text brought her a good laugh. Afterwards, we exchanged texts a few more times that day before returning to our regular routines.

After finishing the audiobook, I received a notification from the person we hired that the Spanish translation had been finished and was ready for viewing. I communicated this information to Hallina, who was instrumental in making it a reality. Hallina shared some more valuable information with me that I wouldn't have known otherwise. She informed me that it's crucial to have several people read a newly translated book before putting it on the market.

I was completely unaware of this beforehand. I was under the impression that once it was translated, it would be ready for distribution. I racked my brain on who to ask. I didn't know many people who met the requirements to read a book written in

Spanish and then whom would be willing to take the time to critique it as well. It dawned on me that Emily and I had met another special person during our Holy Land pilgrimage in early 2020 who might be able to assist us.

This woman traveled to the Holy Land with her mother, which made them yet another mother-daughter duo on the pilgrimage. We bonded with this mother-and-daughter pair for many reasons. The daughter's name was Diana, and like us, she was from the Cedar Rapids area. Diana attended the same church we did, but she attended the Spanish Mass while we went to the English one. Therefore, we had never met each other before prior to that trip.

Diana is a native of Guatemala, and she is proficient in speaking and comprehending Spanish. Initially, I asked her if she could translate the book, but that huge task was a little outside of her comfort zone. Furthermore, it would have taken a considerable amount of time, and she was already very busy attending her son's numerous school and extracurricular activities while also working a full-time job.

I reached out to her and informed her that I had found someone to translate the book. I let her know that actually it was already finished, and I wondered if she would be willing to review it to see if any changes were needed. She stated that she would be happy to do so. Moreover, she informed me that Elfrida, her sister, could also lend a hand. Both of them had a fondness for reading the same books at the same time, attempting to determine who would finish first despite their busy schedules. Diana explained that their competitive nature was beneficial for their relationship, keeping them close and connected in various ways. Furthermore, both are skilled in proofreading translated texts, which would guarantee that the message was clear and not out of context. Their willingness to help us was very much appreciated.

I offered to pay them for their help, but like Hallina, they also refused, saying there was no need because they both loved to read, and the timing for them was perfect. Both of them were extremely willing and helpful in every way.

It turned out that Hallina was correct in her assessment in needing people to proofread the book. Elfrida and Diana discovered numerous errors. Diana mentioned that most of the issues were minor and were the typical errors observed in translated books, such as the alteration of pronouns from female to male. Once they were finished, Emily and I met the two of them for coffee to discuss their thoughts about the book and how these corrections should be properly placed.

Elfrida and Diana spent time reviewing what they found with us. Elfrida gave more guidance on why certain adjustments should be made, pointing out any inconsistencies and even stating the reasons for the modifications. I couldn't believe all the work they each had done. Their thoughtfulness and kindness were truly remarkable.

The four of us had a long conversation about the healings in the book and how, at first, they thought there was no way these stories could be real. It all seemed too good to be true. Diana informed me that she had become quite familiar with me during our nine-day pilgrimage and that she just knew there was no way I would make these stories up.

I shared that, at first, even for us, it was almost unbelievable that stuff like this could exist… and that no one ever told us or showed us over the span of our entire lives. Emily and I both could empathize with her feelings because that's how we originally felt, too.

To be sure that she understood this fact, I stated, "No, I am not making any of it up. Every story, every account that I wrote about, is true."

She smiled and said, "I know it is."

"…I could feel it when I was reading it."

She confided in us that when she was reading the book, sometimes she could literally feel something stirring within herself. She connected this to a sensation that she had only experienced once in her life, and it was during our time together in Israel.

I spoke up and confidently stated, "I know what that was, Diana. That was the Holy Spirit communicating something to you from within your heart about what you were reading."

She agreed, stating that the initial encounter was a result of an experience that involved the Holy Spirit. Diana mentioned that the book really touched her. Instead of me thanking her for all of her help, she was the one to thank us for allowing her to read it. I was taken aback by her sincere words.

Diana informed me later that this book had a significant impact on her life. She shared that she had questioned her purpose for forty-five years, but now, after reading the book, she had gained insight. She expressed her appreciation for me writing this book and sharing my story. It was helping her find the right path in life.

I didn't know what to say. I was incredibly moved by Diana's beautiful comments. I came to the realization that translating the book was a worthwhile investment and effort, even if only one person was affected. It was incredible to think about how God orchestrated all of these events so perfectly. To know that three years earlier, Emily and I met Diana in the Holy Land of all places.

A few weeks after that, I had just given over my second book to the same freelancer on the Fiverr platform to have it translated as well. I waited for the right time and then contacted Diana and Elfrida to see if they were willing to lend a hand once more. Diana was very willing and shared an amazing event that happened to her just a few hours before I reached out to her.

Diana wrote:

> *I have a story to share with you. Last night, at around 1 a.m., a strong smell of flowers woke me up, which scared me because it reminded me of when my grandmother passed away. Then I immediately thought of you and remembered reading about that in your book.*
>
> *So, I took it as a good sign. Then, this morning, I remembered mentioning that I was questioning my life's purpose lately. After reading your book and talking to you and Emily and after much praying and soul searching, I decided that my purpose was to use my knowledge to help senior citizens live a better and healthier life instead of using my ability to make more prominent corporations wealthier.*
>
> *So last month, I decided to change jobs; today was my last day at the insurance company, and I was doubting it was a good idea because next week I start a new job at a start-up company. Being a single mother, I need job security. But you reaching out (today) and allowing me to read your second book, and the smell of flowers tells me that I will be alright. To relax and trust in God.*

My response to Diana's remarkable message:

Wow! I love this!!! Gosh, you know what? I still get doubts about if I am following things correctly as well…all the time. And God uses things like flowers or people in my life to let me know that I'm on the right track, too.

I want to say that I am just so proud of you! That is an amazing leap of faith that you are taking. God will bless you abundantly for it! I am just in awe! And you'll be helping those who need it most!

The fact that I had hired the translator just a few days earlier but knew to wait to reach out to Diana made me realize there was a greater reason for it. In order for her to understand the meaning God was conveying to her through the smell of flowers, the timing of my message was crucial. At that time, I didn't grasp the significance of waiting. All I knew was that I had to follow the sign I was being given.

God's timing was always so perfect.

Isaiah 7:11

"Ask the Lord your God for a sign, whether in the deepest depths or in the highest heights."

nineteen.

IT'S ALL DISTRACTION

I had been dedicating my free time to researching how to obtain nonprofit status and what it would entail. And now, the time was upon us for Emily and me to take those two special people to Ohio for their appointments with Dr. Nemeh.

I had been struggling with things prior to that moment. Despite all the signs God had given me, I still had doubts and questioned both the nonprofit and the upcoming road trip. I felt like there was a battle going on inside my mind. The countless fiery darts being thrown at me to send me off course were beginning to wear me out.

I felt relieved when the day before our trip to Ohio had finally arrived. I was able to relax at that point, knowing the next day the trip would actually take place after all. The following morning, I woke up early to load the car, prepare snacks for the road, feed the dog, and take my morning walk. Emily was already packed, so she didn't need much time to get ready. Therefore, I waited until the last minute to wake her up before it was time to leave and pick up the two women whom God had destined to join us.

As I approached Emily's room, I noticed a faint light coming from under her door, indicating that she was already awake and had turned on her bedside lamp.

She's excited too, I thought, having the false impression the light meant she was already up and ready to go.

I noticed a trash can beside her bed when I opened her bedroom door.

"Uh oh. This is not good," I whispered.

I found Emily propped up in her bed, looking half asleep. She explained that she got sick to her stomach around 3 a.m. but was feeling somewhat better now. She was apologizing and contemplating whether or not she should go just in case it wasn't a fluke and she was really sick.

I asked her, "Well, how do you feel now? You only vomited the one time?"

"Yes, just once, and I feel fine now."

Emily appeared to be alright, even though she felt tired due to the earlier stomach episode that disrupted her sleep.

"Okay, I think you are good. I'll give you a few bites of a banana. It should help you feel better, and we'll be on our way to Cedar Rapids to pick up our two sweet travelers in no time."

While driving, she adamantly insisted that I pull over when we were only two minutes from reaching our destination. As soon as I came to a complete stop, she quickly flung the car door open, and once more, became ill.

We were both devastated. Emily's eyes immediately filled with tears. After that, I don't know how to explain what came over me. All I knew was that I strongly believed this was a test for us.

I asked Emily to get back inside the car and to trust me. I drove for the remaining two minutes until we reached our stopping point. It was clear to me that I needed to talk with the two women accompanying us about our situation. One of them had driven all the way from Kansas City the night before just to be a part of this healing journey. She had gone through so much to come, and I knew that we were not going to let either of them down.

I knew that Emily was aware that I was still contemplating going to Ohio. She had a valid reason for questioning my actions.

"Mom, but what if I am truly sick? We cannot take the risk of that happening. Not for a drive that takes nearly ten hours. And then also potentially infecting everyone else with what I have, too."

I refused to listen. I felt like the Holy Spirit was the driving force behind my thinking, words, and boldness. Although it was amazing, I knew Emily had doubts about what I felt God was telling me.

"You are not contagious, nor are you sick. This is not of God. Someone does not want us to go. I will go inside and speak with these two about everything. Are you okay?"

Emily nodded.

Our car was parked in the driveway while I kept the engine running. I unfastened my seatbelt in a quick-like manner and said, "I will be right back."

"And then what–?" Emily began to question as I left the car and closed the door while she was in mid-sentence.

I ran through the open garage without looking back and tapped on the door. Their luggage was all ready to go, sitting next to the screen door. Then I overheard the woman who lived there talking to her husband about how wonderful the trip was going to be. Upon my knocking, she peeked around the corner and said, "Oh, Christy, good morning! Come on in!"

I remained confident in my plan. I explained the problematic situation and persuaded them to trust me with my suggestion on how to move forward. My friend asked, "Okay, so what are you going to do?"

I replied, "Well, we have some wiggle room, so we don't have to leave right now, as originally planned. We'll wait a bit longer this morning to see how Emily's tummy is progressing since our first appointment with Dr. Nemeh isn't until early tomorrow."

"Right now, I intend to return home, give Emily some water, and pray over her. I'll also reach out to our friend Graeson and see if he can also pray for her, too."

By then, I was surrounded by this woman who was coming on the trip, her husband, and the other woman traveler, who had walked up in the midst of me laying out my plan of action. They were all staring at me as if I had totally lost it.

With a strained smile, I imparted, "She'll be good. I promise. Don't worry, we are still going."

They conversed repeatedly about whether or not they should search for another person to take them to Ohio in case Emily didn't improve. Then they wondered if maybe all Emily needed to do was eat some food to help her feel better. The next thing I knew, they were trying to help by offering to cook her some eggs. Although it was a kind gesture, I was aware that it would not be beneficial. I already knew in my heart what we needed to do.

When I returned to the car, I could tell that Emily was not feeling any better. I informed her about the plan I had put together. She immediately declined, saying, "No. Mom, could you please just take me home? You can take them to Ohio. It's not necessary for me to be there."

"Emily, are you kidding me?" I asked.

"This is our calling. Together. God made us a duo to work together to help people. I can't do this without you."

Despite her efforts to oppose the idea of coming with us, I refused to listen. I immediately grabbed my phone and dialed Graeson's number. The call went straight to voicemail.

I was still being driven by the Holy Spirit, "Graeson, it's Christy. Christy Blake. We need your prayers. This is an emergency!"

Then I laughed out loud, thinking, *This was NOT an emergency!*

"Okay, well, maybe not an emergency," I contradicted, still chuckling at what I said. "We are supposed to be taking these two women to Ohio to see Dr. Nemeh this morning, but Emily has been sick to her stomach. We need prayers. Please pray for her. Please call me."

After hanging up, I let out an audible sigh of frustration, "Ugh."

Emily shook her head, disapproving of how I carried on with this thought. She believed that I was simply being stubborn and not having a realistic outlook. I didn't blame her one bit, especially because she wasn't feeling well. In addition, that is likely what my idea looked like from a normal perspective.

As we pulled into our driveway, my phone rang. It was Graeson.

He apologized for not being able to answer the call. He was at Mass, and his phone was in silent mode.

I told him a little about what had been happening over the past hour or so. Emily continued to be unhappy with the way I was handling things. "I am going inside to lay on the couch," she said while giving me a look as if I was being ridiculous.

I stayed in the car and told Graeson the entire story. After I finished, he said the same thing I said to Emily earlier, "This is not from God, Christy. I just know it. This is the evil one trying to prevent you guys from going on this trip."

"That is exactly what I said!" I told him.

"Christy, is Emily next to you? Is it possible for you to put me on speaker so that I can pray with her?"

"No, she went in the house. I will take you to her, just a minute."

As soon as I walked inside the house, I saw Emily lying on the couch exactly as she had promised moments earlier. I handed her my phone, and Graeson prayed until Emily began to feel better and better.

Graeson was amazing! He told us not to hesitate to reach out if we needed any more prayers or anything at all.

I noticed that Emily felt much better after she hung up, but she wasn't completely 100 percent just yet. My special rosary, the rosary I had brought with me to the Holy Land, came to mind.

During our trip to Israel, we learned that it was permissible to bring rosaries and other holy objects and touch them directly to the authentic Holy Sites. The places where Jesus was born, or the slab of stone that held Christ's body for the anointing are just a few of the examples.

I don't look at my rosary as having special powers. However, I believe it is my faith in those holy places where I touched the rosary that makes my rosary so powerful. When praying with it, I call to mind the significance of those Holy Sites I visited and touched that revolve around the life and death of Christ.

I hurried to the car to retrieve the rosary from my purse.

I placed it on her abdomen and bowed my head, requesting my guardian angel to pray with me. After that, I invoked the Holy Spirit and visualized Jesus working through my touch and healing her. Emily experienced a sensation of heat occurring inside her stomach and more things shifting. After a few minutes, her condition improved even more.

We stayed at the house for another twenty minutes or so until Emily acknowledged that she felt that it was safe to try again.

We collected our friends and their luggage and headed out on the road. To say that our trip was easy after that would be far from the truth. We thought Emily's stomach troubles were completely over, but every now and then, Emily had waves of nausea come around. I would then hand her my rosary, and we would pray it away each time.

The four of us tried to stay focused on believing that everything was going to be okay. Maintaining positive thoughts throughout was challenging because the queasiness continued to reappear. Eventually, we arrived safe and sound in Westlake, Ohio, after nine-plus hours on the road. The amazing thing was that Emily's symptoms disappeared and left for good as soon as we arrived. We were all left speechless after gaining a clearer understanding of what was truly happening.

A priest friend of mine once told me that if a person is being attacked from every angle, there's usually a considerable reason behind it. Typically, the devil is trying to distract them from seeing and receiving the wonderful gift that God has waiting for them just around the corner. It is all distraction. Since I came to know this, I have come to understand how true that statement is. Having this awareness makes it easier for me to calm down in those situations and ask, *Why is this happening? Are there bigger reasons than what meets the eye?*

It was obvious to me that the battle we were engaged in that day was not a physical one, but rather, it was a spiritual one. Despite facing more difficulties during our stay, all four of us saw through the devil's many schemes and understood the importance of staying there, being focused and prayer centered.

Both of the women we brought with us were there for healing. However, the one who faced the most trials on the trip was the person I felt had the most to gain from being there. She had recently been struggling with some significant losses and heartaches in her life, which left her feeling quite sad. Despite the temptation to return home, this woman with a broken heart was able to persevere and stay for her appointment. She appeared to be feeling much better and smiling again within a few hours of her time with Dr. Nemeh.

During the trip, she asked me to speak with her in private. She informed me that she fully grasped the significance of our ministry, stating, "You guys have to keep this going for others." I was grateful that these two women trusted me to keep our plans as they were and join us despite the many uncertainties we endured.

I also had to put my trust in what God had placed in my heart. During Emily's spring break, He opened up two spots for these women in a way that was miraculous. It was meant to be. The blessings that God had in store for those two women were worth the hardships they faced to get there. The power of prayer was evident in every situation we tackled.

Joshua 1:9

Have I not commanded you? Be strong and courageous. Do not be afraid; do not be discouraged, for the Lord your God will be with you wherever you go."

twenty.

INTERCONNECTED

The following month, my entire family went to visit my son, Matthew, and his wife, Allie, at their home in Wisconsin. During that weekend, the two of them informed us that they were expecting. I was ecstatic to learn that I would soon be a grandmother for the first time! The baby was due to be born in November of 2023. This news brought much joy to our entire family!

Easter landed on the following weekend. Due to our recent family gathering, we had fewer family members at our home this year. Only my husband, Randy, Joshua, Emily, and myself were present. The remaining members of the family had other plans. This was the first time my husband and I had such a small gathering in all our time together. Although it weighed on my heart a little, I was still grateful for all the beautiful blessings surrounding me. During the weekend, I had many thoughts about my life and all the changes we've recently witnessed in our family.

It became apparent that my husband was also feeling the effects of some of the same issues. He seemed uninterested in talking and was not his usual self. Randy turned on the television to watch golf. Emily and Josh were watching with him, but I was not as interested. I decided to collect the dishes from our Easter meal and put them in the sink to be washed later when I felt more like myself.

I opted to go sit outside on our deck and spend some time with God. I was sharing my thoughts and heart with Him. I was so excited about the news about the new grandchild, but even so, I still felt somewhat sad that they didn't live closer. It seemed wrong to be unhappy about anything after everything God had done in my life.

Despite my unsuccessful efforts to overcome my sadness, I was also unclear about many things in my future. I was contemplating whether I was supposed to be searching for a job to help pay our bills or what I was meant to be doing. I was experiencing a lot of confusion at that moment. My mind was spinning while I was thinking about these thoughts and more, when I was suddenly reminded of all the times I felt God leading me to write this third book. For months now, I've been receiving signs, nudges, and dreams that I need to be writing this book. A book that I hadn't even started yet or knew how to begin.

Had I really been given signs? I wondered. *Was I thinking that God was calling me to do another book, but in reality, that part of my life was all over and done with now?*

I had tears in my eyes. I was sad that I was confused. I was even sad that I was sad. Ugh!

I was confronted with the same questions I had before, *How would I write about my son's healing story in this book?*

The process of blending the stories surrounding Dr. Nemeh with Joshua's story that involved Graeson was a mystery to me. They seemed like two different worlds, and I just couldn't see how they all fit together. I was overwhelmed trying to connect everything together. I found myself in a familiar setting, experiencing frustration with my thoughts and doubts.

Once again, I was seeking another sign from God to help guide me. "If you are asking me to do this, and this third book is truly meant to be written... please give me a sign."

After gazing up into the sky, I let my prayer drift in the air for a moment before hopping off our porch swing and returning inside the house.

I went back inside and grabbed a drink of water from the refrigerator. I was trying to shrug off my sadness and insecurities and trusting God to show me the way. Within a few minutes, my mind was already preoccupied with other things. The television was still the focus of everyone else's attention. I decided to go sit with the others in the living room and drink my water before starting my chores. I settled into a comfortable position on the couch and removed my phone from my pocket. It came to my attention that I had received a message from Facebook Messenger a few minutes earlier.

Upon opening Messenger, I was taken aback by the person who sent it. I received a message from Dr. Issam Nemeh!

It read, "Happy Easter to You and Yours. God Bless."

I have never received any messages from Dr. Nemeh in the several years I've known him. Not once. I was utterly captivated by this, and then it hit me. This was THE sign. The notification, being about four minutes old, made me think it came right after I said the prayer on the deck.

I was in total awe!

Compiling all of these stories together was still a challenge for me. I came back to the fact that God had responded to me the last time I asked Him about it. He conveyed to me that all the miracles, healings, and beauty are attributed to Him and Him alone. And that was all that mattered. The only thing I needed to do was to trust that this was about spreading the message about how He ministers through others to reach those in need. The whole objective is to get people to return to Him wholeheartedly. The purpose and message of writing this book is to educate people about what He's doing and why. The emphasis is not on who God is actively working through but rather on His effort to reach a significant number of people at this time.

A month had passed, and I still hadn't started writing yet because I had some things to finish up first. After submitting all the required information to the IRS for *The Blessed Reason Trip*, we were officially granted nonprofit status. I was updating our website and displaying the new changes. In addition to that, I was in the process of designing a website for our other organization, *Mission of Mercy Magnified*.

During this time, I was introduced to a young woman who was seeking healing. She was interested in seeing Dr. Nemeh and wanted to speak with me, hear my testimony, and learn more. We had a lengthy conversation, and I offered to send her both of my books in the mail to read.

As the conversation came to a close, she informed me that her grandfather was also listening on the phone. At that moment, he spoke up and thanked me for sharing my story with them. He said, "I think you and your daughter have a big role in the end times by what you are doing."

I replied, "Ah, thank you, but no, our main purpose is to educate people about Dr. Nemeh and how they can find God's healing through his prayers. Our goal is to reconnect people's souls to God through this process."

The next morning, I told my husband what this kind grandfather had said to me. I said, "It was such a nice thing to say, but he had it all wrong. We are just following what God has put on our hearts," I elaborated.

To which Randy replied, "I think you guys have a much bigger role than you think." Then, he just gave me a kiss and went to leave for work as if what he said was no big deal. I, however, was completely caught off guard by his comment. I was moved to tears because those were not the types of things my husband typically said or discussed.

Later, I was reflecting on some of the setbacks and trials I encountered while working for the *Mission of Mercy Magnified* organization with Emily and Sue. It occurred to me that this new organization is also connected to helping people discover God. The foundation of this mission is the Corporal Works of Mercy and how Jesus asks us to serve Him, particularly in Matthew chapter 25.

Matthew 25: 35-45 NIV

For I was hungry and you gave me something to eat, I was thirsty and you gave me something to drink, I was a stranger and you invited me in, I needed clothes and you clothed me, I was sick and you looked after me, I was in prison and you came to visit me.'

"Then the righteous will answer him, 'Lord, when did we see you hungry and feed you, or thirsty and give you something to drink? When did we see you a stranger and invite you in, or needing clothes and clothe you? When did we see you sick or in prison and go to visit you?'

"The King will reply, 'Truly I tell you, whatever you did for one of the least of these brothers and sisters of mine, you did for me.'

"Then he will say to those on his left, 'Depart from me, you who are cursed, into the eternal fire prepared for the devil and his angels. For I was hungry and you gave me nothing to eat, I was thirsty and you gave me nothing to drink, I was a stranger and you did not invite me in, I needed clothes and you

did not clothe me, I was sick and in prison and you did not look after me.'

"They also will answer, 'Lord, when did we see you hungry or thirsty or a stranger or needing clothes or sick or in prison, and did not help you?'

"He will reply, 'Truly I tell you, whatever you did not do for one of the least of these, you did not do for me.'

It is believed that the Last and Final Judgment is the culmination of the actions we take or fail to take in life to help others. Compiling information on how to serve the community and educating people about the significance of doing so serves a dual purpose. It is beneficial to both the recipient and to those who are serving. In other words, those who assist others are being blessed in the process.

When I looked at the bigger picture, I realized how everything was interconnected.

2 Corinthians 5:10

For we must all appear before the judgment seat of Christ, so that each of us may receive what is due us for the things done while in the body, whether good or bad.

twenty-one.

CORN CHIPS & GOOD COMPANY

I shared the new changes regarding *The Blessed Reason Trip* with Kathy Nemeh. She shared in our joy for the unique way the Lord was leading us. I put in a lot of effort for weeks to revamp our website, making sure to mention that anyone who supported our organization could now receive a tax-deductible receipt. Once I was finished working on it, I forwarded our freshly designed site to Kathy. I wanted to make sure she felt comfortable with how I presented our organization's mission of helping people get to Ohio.

Kathy was fond of our new setup, but unfortunately, I had not grasped that the Lord was leading us to a more expansive path. And because of that, we now had an issue with the way I presented our purpose. Since we were granted nonprofit status, we had to diversify our organization and not only focus on Dr. Nemeh. Otherwise, there would be a significant conflict of interest. I didn't realize that becoming a nonprofit would have such a drastic impact on our mission. Furthermore, I had to start all over again on the website. The site that I had just spent so much time building.

I have no words to express my disappointment. It was unclear to me why God had brought me to this point. I had believed that by becoming a nonprofit, we could assist more individuals in finding healing through Dr. Nemeh. Now, it appeared to be the exact opposite.

Upon further research, it became evident that we cannot demonstrate favoritism towards any individual or organization as a nonprofit. My next few days were filled with many tears. I was trying to figure out what happened and what to do next.

Kathy Nemeh comprehended the extent to which our hearts were dedicated to telling others about our miracles and, likewise, those we had witnessed around us. She understood why we had made it our life's mission to inform everyone about her husband and the miraculous ways that God works through his prayers.

Kathy was trying to help me through the situation by sharing that changing our website and focus really wasn't that big of a deal. Although I knew it wasn't, it still deeply affected me.

I texted Kathy, "Gosh, I am sorry to make a mess of things. I am going to pray my way through how to rearrange it. Thank you for always being so helpful and loving."

Kathy's response was, "No mess at all."

"Just technical stupid stuff."

It took me a little longer to overcome this setback. I was filled with sadness and believed that I had been tricked into believing that we should be a nonprofit. I replayed that incident at church where Lisa DeWees squeezed my arm right when I called out for a sign. Playing that off as merely a coincidence was tough, especially since I had only met her once, two years earlier.

I was striving to move forward and observe the direction of things. I thought about canceling our nonprofit in the back of my mind. *Is that even possible?* I questioned.

I made the decision to organize a board meeting in late June to gather the opinions of everyone else on the matter. We gathered at a local Mexican restaurant, to discuss how to proceed with these new changes. Emily and I shared our unique nonprofit situation with the other two board members and sought their advice on how to proceed. Even after listening to their insights and guidance, I was still unsure what this meant for our future.

Just as we were about to leave, Lisa DeWees, the angel who squeezed my arm, came walking by. Upon seeing us, she turned around and proceeded to approach our table. She talked to us about the power of prayer and the fact that her husband was about to become an official deacon in the Catholic church.

Then Lisa asked the question, "Christy, weren't you launching a nonprofit to educate people about healing prayers?"

We shared the story with the rest of our group about that particular day in church, where she terrified me greatly when she squeezed my arm. Our table was filled with laughter as a result of that story. And now, here we were, having our first board meeting because Lisa was the one who helped me move forward in faith. Despite the doubts I had recently been dealing with the past few weeks, this moment lifted my spirits significantly.

I told her my dilemma about rearranging our website and being at a loss about how our organization should proceed. I conveyed to Lisa that I had been contemplating the origins of our nonprofit. I said, "It literally all started with your famous arm squeeze. And here we are at our first board meeting, and we ran into you once again."

"Another divine intervention, no doubt," I added.

Lisa then proceeded to give me one affirmation after another, telling me that what I was doing was right and to believe in it. She said she could see it play a more prominent role in the future. I expressed my gratitude for her kind words. Next, she began discussing all the healing services that had been emerging in the area. The timing was remarkable, showing the extent of God's effort to reach His people.

Lisa told us about a few of the new ministries and offered to share more details about them with us.

She suggested that our site could provide a wide range of opportunities for people to find healing. Ultimately, we would still be doing the same thing, leading people to finding God in their lives.

God orchestrated something beautiful once more to assist me in discovering ways to move forward. It was made clear that the purpose of this website was to list the many ways in which individuals can find healing. We would provide a list of different prayer service options around us. At last, I found peace and believed that God would give us additional guidance on how to move forward.

As we are located in Iowa and have knowledge of various healing options, I began listing prayer service options in our local area. We now have two different pages of healing ministries listed on our website. The first page is devoted to Iowa, while the second covers other ministries throughout the nation. Dr. Nemeh's prayer services are included on the list, with a link to his *Path to Faith* website provided.

My discovery is that our goal has largely remained the same. We are to keep promoting God's healing through the various healing ministries that have become widely available. Ultimately, we retain the hope that God's healing will lead people into a closer relationship with Jesus.

From the very beginning, that has been God's plan. We all have a responsibility to evangelize and share the Good News with others.

Psalm 32:8

I will instruct you and teach you in the way you should go;
I will counsel you with my loving eye on you.

twenty-two.

CONNECTING THE DOTS

It would be reasonable to assume that by now, I would have a lot of things figured out in my life after all that I had recently been through and that it would be much easier for me to discern how to follow the Lord. Unfortunately, this has not been the case for me. Not at all. Our family faced some uncertainties and scares in the middle of 2023. Due to these circumstances, I found myself going down an all too familiar path once more. And while it's embarrassing to confess these things, I understand the value of doing so because we can learn from one another.

In late June, I became consumed with worry regarding some family issues. It wasn't long before I found myself lost yet again. I was not praying like I should and was pretty much entirely fixated on the problems at hand with constant worrying. I'm not implying that I wasn't praying. I was. I just wasn't doing it the right way. I was constantly praying, but mostly begging for things to be fixed, without really focusing my attention on Him, His love, or even my love for Him.

After going through that awful period when I started to feel sick like I used to, I truly believed I would never move away from Him again. Despite the lessons I had learned, I was still unable to stay on course in the face of life's challenges. I was once again failing to do what I was supposed to be doing.

After several weeks of my energy levels tanking and feeling so sick, I began to worry that something was seriously wrong with me. At some point, I realized that I had done it again. I had once again slipped up.

I began to pray with all my heart, searching for His closeness and love for the first time in weeks as soon as I became aware of this. The weakness, tiredness, and pain that was starting to come back disappeared immediately after I did that. It's a mystery to me how I managed to forget this lesson every time something came up.

I was definitely witnessing a pattern. Whenever there were any distractions or troubles in my life, I would neglect praying, spending time with the Lord, or following His will for my life. My entire body would begin to completely shut down as a result. I had no idea that I had drifted off course until I got sick.

Eventually, I would come to terms with my mistakes, redirect, and reconnect with Him. For some strange reason, I couldn't connect the dots between not feeling well and my drifting away until things got so bad that they were concerning, sometimes even scary. I was feeling annoyed with myself and quite honestly, was beginning to worry about my memory. *How could I constantly get so distracted and forget?*

My daughter Emily had a profound dream in the vicinity of this time. In it, she asked Dr. Nemeh a question. "How do you stop distracting thoughts?"

His response to her in the dream was basically to trust God with her mind. "Give God control of your mind. They are either your thoughts or God's."

When Emily shared this with me, I was taken aback by the timing, simplicity, and truthfulness of that statement. Despite it being only a dream, it made complete sense.

I was sharing Emily's dream with my dear friend Kathy Connolly. Kathy's many incredible healings are documented in my second book. Her visit to Dr. Nemeh in 2020 saved her life and healed her from RSD and other life-threatening health issues. Kathy told me she had recently been thinking about something

Dr. Nemeh had said during one of the Zoom calls. She recalled him saying, "The best healings are the ones of the mind."

During that time, she heard a priest discussing how to determine if your thoughts were yours or God's. The priest explains that you won't know for sure if you're not taking time to be in the Word. Hence, Kathy stated that she was in the process of searching for a Study Bible due to her recent desire to gain a better understanding of where her thoughts were coming from. Her goal was to read the Word daily with the intention of hearing His voice more clearly. We couldn't believe the funny timing since we were also discerning about this same concept, and then Emily had that dream. In addition to everything else, Emily and I also recently bought Study Bibles for ourselves. It seemed as if God was constantly revealing more ways for us to be closer to Him.

While working hard on redesigning *The Blessed Reason Trip's* website, I remembered a statement made by Lisa DeWees during our previous conversation. She was speaking about a group of local priests who have recently come together to hold their own healing services every three months. I had heard about this new ministry twice now in recent weeks. Lisa gave me the name of one of the priests. She believed that adding this ministry to our website's new layout would be beneficial.

Emily and I were able to reach this priest and have a conversation about their ministry and the possibility of adding them in. During our discussion, we learned that there were a total of eight priests who felt called by the Holy Spirit to bring this to our neighboring communities. For nearly an hour, we conversed with him about how God was recently opening doors and revealing Himself to so many people. The entire conversation was uplifting from start to finish.

During our discussion, in the back of my mind, I was still thinking about all the tasks I felt called to complete. I was wondering if they were truly from the Lord when the priest made a profound statement about how God works. He said that if someone answers and responds to God's calls, He will keep calling us, assigning more tasks for us to do for Him. The priest's theory was validated by our daily lives; likewise, his words made me feel better about the overall direction of our paths over the last few years.

I was attempting to follow God's lead during the conversation, listening for His guidance on what to say. When, out of nowhere, the priest commented about something that I'm not sure he fully grasped the overall impact it had on me at the time. He said that he could literally feel the Holy Spirit coming through my words during our conversation. The priest's words on that day significantly affirmed that I was truly hearing God's voice.

He spent some time informing Emily and me about other Catholic healing ministries that he believed were highly reputable and should be listed on our website. At the end of our conversation, he expressed that his intention was to speak with the other seven priests about being included as well. I'm still waiting to hear back, but I understand that their schedules are extremely busy. To hear back from a total of eight priests could potentially take a while.

To conclude our conversation, he graciously asked if he could pray for our own ministry. He spoke about Mark 4:20 and Matthew 13:8. He discussed the seeds that fall on fertile soil and produce "more." Some yielded thirtyfold, some sixtyfold, and others yielded one hundredfold of what was planted.

The priest asked God to bless our ministry, helping it to grow to its fullest potential, just like the one who harvested one hundredfold in the Gospel story. He invited us to their next mission so that he could introduce himself and the other priests to us in person.

Later that same afternoon, Emily and I talked to a deacon from Dubuque, Iowa, who also had a healing ministry. Lisa DeWees provided us with information about this person, too. Our conversation focused on who we were and how God healed us through the prayers of a special doctor in Ohio. This healing completely transformed us into who we are today, and we wanted others to know that it is available to them too. We let him know about our new nonprofit status and our reasoning for wanting to add healing ministries like his to our website.

It was quite a thrilling day for us. Additionally, we added *Prairie Fire Ministries* to our website, the ministry that Graeson was associated with. I was starting to see that the many things God was calling me to do were, in one way or another, all connected in such a perfect way.

Romans 15:5-6

May the God who gives endurance and encouragement give you the same attitude of mind toward each other that Christ Jesus had, so that with one mind and one voice you may glorify the God and Father of our Lord Jesus Christ.

twenty-three.

THERE'S NO LIMIT

In August 2023, I was experiencing a strange sensation in my throat. This was the second time that this had occurred. The first time was nearly two months earlier when I was home by myself. I experienced a sudden pain while working on one of the websites. The pain was sharp and stabbing, and it occurred repeatedly. It was so bad that I could hardly bear it. The peculiar aspect was that it was situated inside my neck and throat.

I could not understand what was happening or why. The pain was so intense that I couldn't move. I wanted to scream, but I couldn't even do that. The only thing I could do was to pray to

God for help. Initially, I thought I was experiencing an aneurysm or something similar. I literally thought I was going to die.

Jesus, PLEASE! Help me, I prayed from my heart. The pain was so intense that I couldn't speak a word. *Guardian angel, help me,* again insistently praying...begging.

The pain persisted. I prayed to the Blessed Mother, *Hail Mary, full of grace, the Lord is with thee….St. Pio, PLEASE!*

Then, as quickly as it began, it stopped. My body was shaking from the pain and terror that gripped me. My heart was beating violently in my chest. I rubbed the front of my neck in total disbelief at what just happened. I sat there for a minute trying to comprehend when all of a sudden, I just started crying.

I began to cry with such intensity that I was sobbing. I was finding it challenging to collect myself.

I could not figure out what in the world just happened to me. I questioned, *Could that have been some sort of spiritual attack?*

I figured it had to have been. *If it were a real physical issue, it wouldn't have just stopped like it did…Right?*

To me, the pain was so severe that if there had been a physical reason for it, it would have been fatal. After some time, I was able to gather myself and regroup. I prayed, grateful to God for rescuing me from whatever just happened. As I glanced at the clock, I became aware that Randy and Emily were going to be coming home from work in a few hours. I thought about whether or not I should share this with either of them.

I knew instantly that I wouldn't reveal anything to Randy. If it were something spiritual, the topic would make him feel uncomfortable. At that point, I was certain that I wouldn't share it with Emily either. She would be freaked out if it were something spiritual. Heck, I was freaked out by it! It was still a mystery to me what could have caused something like that. It was just so strange.

I attempted to find a physical explanation for about a minute but quickly dismissed it. I thought there was no way. If so, I believed it would have to be an extremely severe medical condition, and since I now felt fine, I didn't think that could be the case. So, I kept silent, not telling anyone. I did my best to put it out of my mind, and within a few days, I pretty much had forgotten all about it.

However, in mid-August, it occurred again when I was on my way to pick up our dog from the kennel where he was being cared for in a neighboring town. I came upon a construction zone on the highway. They were working on the bridge that spans a nearby local river, narrowing it down to one lane. I was waiting in traffic for the stop light to turn green so we could cross over. I suddenly experienced it coming on again. Immediately, the pain intensified, giving me perhaps a one-second warning to go from no pain to the worst I've ever had in my life.

I couldn't move. I was worried that my foot would come off the brake. The intense pain almost paralyzed my brain from processing anything else, even though I wanted to scream. I was only attempting to cope.

The duration was roughly the same as the previous one. Although it was probably only a minute long, it felt like an eternity. After it was over, the light turned green, allowing traffic to continue on its way. I was trying not to bawl my eyes out as I was driving. It was just so painful, overwhelming, and terrifying that I couldn't help but cry. The only way I made it to the boarding kennel was through prayer. Once I arrived, I am pretty sure that I set a new world record for the fastest dog pick-up ever.

As I made my way back home, I was filled with fear. I didn't understand what was happening to me. When I returned to the house, I again kept this entirely to myself. Before speaking to anyone about it, I wanted to do some research first. I still had no clue what was going on.

During my research, I came across a condition that resembled what I had just gone through. "Stabbing, electric shock pains either in the throat, around the ear, neck...and the typical age of onset is someone in their fifties." It accurately reflected what I had experienced, and my age was also within the typical parameters.

I meticulously examined everything, from the cause to the right kind of doctor to consult about this condition. It didn't sound great, with most people describing it as only worsening in the upcoming months and years ahead, leading to more frequent occurrences.

It seemed that I needed to visit a neurosurgeon and request CT scans to obtain an affirmative diagnosis. All I knew was that I never wanted to go through that experience again in my entire life. My heart was heavy when I went to sleep that night.

The next morning, I continued researching until I became sick with worry. I decided to send an email to my husband about everything while he was at work. I gave him links that described what it likely was and patients who shared their experiences that were quite similar to mine. I thought that he would investigate it further and we would discuss it when he got home.

I contacted Dr. Nemeh's office directly after sending that email. I inquired about an immediate Facetime virtual prayer session while also arranging an office medical appointment for a day that was already scheduled for Emily to have off from work, Friday, October 27th. I wanted to make sure that I had scheduled an office appointment, just in case. The thought of going through this painful experience again was extremely frightening for me. Therefore, I was making every effort to prevent it from happening again.

After inquiring with Dr. Nemeh's office, I received a text from my husband stating, "Maybe you could have a remote appointment with Dr. Nemeh."

I replied that I had just asked for one. About a minute later, Dr. Nemeh's office informed me that they were able to miraculously place me on the schedule for a virtual prayer that same weekend. It was to be in just a few days, on Saturday, August 19th. I was extremely thankful and feeling more confident that everything would eventually be okay.

Next, I knew that I had to inform Emily when she came home from teaching. I sat her down at our desk in the living room and told her that something was not right with me. Emily expressed instant concern and said, "I knew something was wrong last night. You weren't yourself at all. You were so quiet and went to bed early."

I apologized but explained that I was still in the process of trying to figure it all out.

"Figure what out?"

I turned the computer chair around and pulled up the email I had sent to her father hours earlier. I requested that she read it. It would be easier for me to not have to explain and relive the entire story again.

After carefully reading the document, she highlighted the condition I mentioned, copied and pasted it into a web browser, and attempted to investigate the severity of the situation on her own. I informed her that after sending that email, I was blessed to learn that I was added to Dr. Nemeh's schedule for the upcoming Saturday. I told her that I also set up an office appointment with him on her day off in late October. "I want you there with me, Emily," I said with tears filling my eyes.

She became emotional, too, after reading about the terrifying symptoms I had experienced. "Mom, Dr. Nemeh will pray, and Jesus will take care of you. You will be okay, I know it."

"I know. But I am wondering how many miracles can a person ask for," I stated, as my tears increased.

"There is no limit, Mom. We simply hand everything over to Him. And just trust. It's that simple."

I knew she was right. If it were someone else, I would say the same thing to them. However, when it came to talking about myself, I didn't see things in the same light for some reason. I felt very unworthy to be continually asking, over and over again. In truth, I knew that the number of times was irrelevant. God's love for us far surpasses anything we can comprehend. He wants us always to come to Him, no matter the issue.

Matthew 11:28

"Come to me, all you who are weary and burdened, and I will give you rest.

twenty-four.

THE GOOD NEWS

When it was time for the virtual call on Saturday, Emily was ready to be there for me. She brought two chairs over to her computer desk. We sat down next to each other, waiting for the call to connect. She lovingly stayed with me, holding my hand and praying for me. During the appointment, I provided Dr. Nemeh with an explanation of what I had been experiencing. His initial inquiry was: "What did your doctor say?"

I was embarrassed to reply, "I haven't seen one."

I could see the look on his face. He wasn't too thrilled with my answer. While Dr. Nemeh is a man who has a faith that is unmatched, he also acknowledges that God and science are inseparable. He views them in the same way that our spirit and body are interwoven.

I continued giving more details about my situation while trying to overlook his apparent disappointment that I hadn't seen a local physician about it.

"Well, actually, I kept it to myself the first time it happened. I was pretty scared. I didn't know if it was some spiritual attack," to which Doctor immediately shook his head, '*No*.'

I continued, "The second time just happened last Sunday, six days ago."

Dr. Nemeh questioned, "Are you self-diagnosing yourself, Christy?"

I chuckled nervously and softly responded, "Yes."

Dr. Nemeh replied, "That is dangerous. You should never do that."

Despite my internet research, he disagreed with my conclusion and asserted that my neck was the cause of these peculiar and unpleasant sensations. As soon as I heard him say that, it dawned on me that I was also feeling a peculiar discomfort on the back of my neck, similar to a pinched nerve. It had been bothering me for some time, but I hadn't paid much attention to it until then.

I have discovered that old injuries to my neck have been the primary source of most of my health problems, both in the past and presently. Dr. Nemeh has informed me that neck and/or spinal injuries are frequently linked to many health problems.

Dr. Nemeh began to pray and, after a few minutes, inquired if I felt anything. It took me a minute or two to assess whether I had felt anything or not. I was aware that this was a normal occurrence, as he typically feels it before the person he's praying for does.

But I *could* feel it! The Holy Spirit was present. I was encountering a substantial amount of heat on the back of my neck. It was beginning to diminish the tenderness that I felt. The funny thing was, I wasn't even aware of having it until Dr. Nemeh pointed out that my unusual symptoms originated from my neck. And then just like that, all the sensitivity and soreness began to fade away.

Dr. Nemeh reassured me that what I had was only a physical issue and not a spiritual one. That was a huge relief! Honestly, the idea of it possibly being spiritual almost scared me more than the pain itself. After praying for me, Doctor asked us how we were doing otherwise. Emily shared about the upcoming arrival of Matt's baby in November and that she was very excited to become an aunt.

It was touching to me that we were sitting and talking to Dr. Nemeh in that way, even for only a few minutes. Here we were, conversing with this incredible man of faith, just chatting about life. He was always there to assist us in connecting with Jesus throughout many of our trials in life. We feel extremely blessed to be able to call someone so exceptional a close and dear friend. A friend through Christ. The way God connected us with the Nemehs was truly beautiful.

I couldn't believe how well the prayer had gone. While I was aware that my neck is usually the cause of many of my other problems, I was not expecting that to be the case this time. However, I shouldn't have been that surprised, considering as a child, my brother and I fell out of a moving vehicle. We rolled out of the car and down the highway at incredible speeds for quite a while before my mom realized what had transpired.

I was unaware that this childhood injury would end up being the cause of so many problems later on in life. Until one day in 2019, Dr. Nemeh mentioned that I had suffered a pretty bad neck injury at some point in my life. It didn't take long for me to put two and two together. That childhood injury is directly related to many of my current neurological symptoms, including my migraines. I was so thankful that my recent painful and scary incidents were easily attributed to this same injury and could be prayed away.

After we chatted for a bit, we let Dr. Nemeh get back to his busy schedule and start praying for the others he had waiting. The next day, Sunday, August 20th, the *Path to Faith* monthly Zoom Healing Service was held. Jessica, the lady who typically gives instructions on how the event will proceed, made a moving comment during our attendance. She observed that it was time for us to gather once again for our favorite time of the month - the time when we were with our *Path to Faith "Family."* She was absolutely correct. In every sense of the word, it truly felt like we were with family!

My son Joshua arrived at our door approximately twenty minutes into the Zoom. He didn't know what we were doing and was just dropping by to say "hello." We invited him to stay and sit with us to watch and participate in this special monthly event. He seemed quite happy to oblige and be there with us.

Before the healing prayers begin in the meetings, Dr. Nemeh usually answers questions from participants. This time, someone inquired when the in-person healing services would resume. I noticed Kathy looked pretty excited and looked at Doc for the answer.

Dr. Nemeh mentioned that they still had to be cautious, but they were looking into the possibilities of trying to bring them back. I was so excited that I almost jumped out of my seat. Wow! I had no idea that they were thinking about bringing them back. Although I knew no promises were made and they were only looking into it, the excitement was still there.

Dr. Nemeh discussed the importance of holding them, noting that when people witness someone around them experience healing, their belief and faith are further strengthened. Then, more healings begin to occur. In addition, he stressed the importance of everyone being there to pray for each other, saying that our prayers become so powerful.

I hurried downstairs to inform my husband that the Nemehs were considering this. "No promises," I warned, "but still... It is just so exciting!"

He asked, "Does that mean more bus trips?"

I laughed and started running back up the stairs to get back to the meeting. I called out, slightly short of breath from running to and fro, "I don't know. I am not really thinking about that right now. I am just so excited about the possibility of the Nemehs bringing the healing services back... This is so HUGE!"

I could hear my husband chuckling at my excitement as I ran out of sight.

Kathy recounted a miraculous story about a young baby boy at the end of the service. She stated that he was sick, and doctors had given him only two to four months to live. He couldn't eat on his own and barely moved. The doctors had to insert a feeding tube. The mother was desperate and brought him into the office for treatment and prayer. Kathy held up her phone to the camera, displaying a video to everyone in the Zoom meeting about what happened when Dr. Nemeh prayed over him.

The mother was shown sitting in a chair while holding her baby outstretched in her arms. The baby lay in a state of complete stillness with its eyes closed, unaware of its surroundings. Dr. Nemeh approached and placed his hand over the baby's chest. A few seconds later, the baby's eyes opened.

This child's awakening continued. He began to shift his eyes, looking around a bit here and there. The position of Dr. Nemeh's hand remained unchanged. The baby's alertness increased by the second. Then, the baby shifted its attention to Dr. Nemeh, gazing upward into his eyes. For seconds, Dr. Nemeh and the baby stared at each other in the most loving way possible. As I was watching this, I was shedding tears and witnessed many others on the screen doing the same during the virtual call.

Kathy Nemeh mentioned that the mother would be returning to the Mayo Clinic for a reevaluation. However, after witnessing that incredible moment, she felt confident that she had nothing to worry about any longer. Shortly after the prayer from Dr. Nemeh, the baby began feeding from a bottle. He was unable to do this before. The video was a powerful reminder of what can happen through prayer. I was incredibly thankful that Kathy shared this beautiful moment with everyone.

After the service, I relayed what we observed to several others who were not present during the call. It was truly remarkable! At first, the child was listless, appearing almost nonresponsive. The child seemed to come back to life as Dr. Nemeh held out his hand and prayed. What took place defies any physical or logical explanation. From my perspective, it was clear that God was connecting the baby's spirit and Dr. Nemeh's spirit together.

Furthermore, I believe that the video helped anyone who had doubts during that service to believe in God's ability to do anything!

1 John 5:14-15

This is the confidence we have in approaching God: that if we ask anything according to His will, He hears us. And if we know that He hears us—whatever we ask—we know that we have what we asked of Him.

twenty-five.

SEE YOU SOON!

After the virtual service was over, Joshua, Emily, and I were discussing that special moment with the prayer over the baby when I asked Joshua a question.

"Have you read my first book yet?"

He glanced down at the floor. I knew the answer. I wasn't upset. And the funny thing was I didn't even intend to ask him anything. It appeared to come out of thin air. My belief is that the Holy Spirit was guiding me to prepare him for what this third book would contain: a piece of his story.

Before I knew it, I asked another, "How about my second book? Have you read that?"

He shifted awkwardly in his chair and shook his head, saying, "No."

I let him know that was okay. I understood he had a hectic schedule. When Joshua could see I wasn't upset by this, he breathed a sigh of relief.

I offered to give him the audiobook link. That way, he could listen to me read the story while he was driving or working with his earbuds in, "Just like when you were younger, and I would read to you every night," I said.

He smirked, smiled, and thoughtfully said, "That actually sounds really nice."

On Monday, August 28th, one week later, I woke up from another remarkable dream. Dr. Nemeh appeared in it, greeting me with a warm "hello" and a hug. We were on our way to his car while conversing as we walked. On the way, I shared with him how much he meant to me and Emily and how much we both loved him. We walked at a leisurely pace, discussing all the special ways the Holy Spirit connects people, and because of him, our lives were now so different.

Dr. Nemeh chuckled and acknowledged that he felt it too, revealing that it was our connection with Jesus that made this possible. As soon as we reached his car, I pulled out a stack of three books I had been carrying while walking and handed them all over to him. We both gazed at the top book for a moment until he looked up, smiled, and extended another hug to me. After placing the books in the back seat, he opened the driver's door, entered the car, glanced over at me, and said, "I'll see you soon."

Then, he proceeded to drive away while I stood there by myself in the parking lot...alone with my thoughts.

I was filled with questions as he drove away. *What did that mean...See you soon?*

Although I was searching for answers, I was still asleep and dreaming. I was trying to understand what Dr. Nemeh meant by that statement. When I asked the meaning of it, the date "October 27th“ came to mind right away. At once, I gained a better understanding of what the entire dream meant.

I was aware that the appointment I initially scheduled for myself regarding those scary, painful incidents was on that same date. And on that day of the appointment, I would be handing over my completed third book to Dr. Nemeh. I knew the book's content would cover the variety of ways in which Jesus has answered prayers, as well as some vital knowledge that I have learned from Dr. Nemeh over the past few years.

Upon contemplating whether I still needed the appointment, I heard in my heart again while still dreaming, "You are healed. The appointment is not meant for you."

I asked, "Then, who is the appointment for?"

I was awakened by the sight of my son's face rushing toward me.

The more I came to, the more I became awestruck by what had just occurred. I glanced at my phone, and it was 5:00 a.m. Every morning for the past few days, I've been waking up at this time. Regardless of how late I went to bed, I was awakened from sleep at five o'clock. I saw it as a wake-up call from the Holy Spirit and used that extra time each morning to spend with Jesus before starting my day.

The fact that I woke up at the exact same time brought me joy, particularly given the dream I had just had.

I revisited the entire dream again, dissecting each part to examine and verify that it was not a typical dream. My dreams always seemed to have a special message attached to them whenever Kathy or Dr. Nemeh appeared in them, and this one wasn't any different.

In my dream, I gave Dr. Nemeh three books. Although I couldn't see the names of the books, I knew what they were. All of them were written by me. The first book that I wrote was the one at the bottom. The middle was my second one. While examining the top of the stack, I was shocked to see it was a book that I had just finished writing, also known as this one I am writing right now.

When I realized that it was my third book, I was stunned. I stared at it in disbelief, but Doctor seemed to glance at it with a slight hint of recognition in his eyes, as though he already knew about it. Suddenly, I grasped the fact that the appointment was approaching fast. It was less than two months away. Anxiety started creeping up on me. *How can I write an entire book in such a short period of time?* I wondered.

As soon as I had these worries, I felt a sense of certainty emerge over me that it could *somehow* be accomplished. Although I was still nervous about writing an entire book so quickly, I believed that God would help me if this was truly a divine dream. I had faith that the Holy Spirit would assist me in writing it.

I was still uncertain about what to make of Joshua's face coming to me, and I was curious why he would need an appointment with Dr. Nemeh. I eventually hopped out of bed and thanked the Lord for such a beautiful and amazing dream, asking Him to show me the way. After taking time to pray some more, I proceeded with my day as usual.

After making lunches for my husband and daughter's workday, I gave our dog his morning walk about half an hour later. While on that walk, the Lord reminded me of a dream He had given me a year earlier. It was the dream where God had shown me the entire conversation that I would have with my son Joshua beforehand, including the time and location. I wrote earlier in this book about the message that was associated with that dream. That being, Josh's heart would soften, and this healing would stay with him for the rest of his life. However, there was more to that dream that I had dismissed at the time. And up until now, I had forgotten all about it. The dream ended with Emily and I taking Joshua to Ohio for an appointment with Dr. Nemeh.

I initially dismissed the last portion because I thought that he wouldn't need to see Dr. Nemeh again. *Oh my gosh!*

I couldn't believe it! *Everything* in that dream from last year really has come to fruition!

I came to a standstill on our gravel lane, totally overwhelmed by everything I had been shown, both last year and now. *Why did I doubt the last part of that dream when I had it?* I asked myself.

Right then, I knew for certain that we would be taking Joshua to Ohio for that appointment on October 27th. There were reasons it was for Josh that I just wasn't aware of yet. I also knew that I could no longer deny that I would be writing this third book. A book I had hardly even given much thought to starting until that moment. Now, I had less than two months to write, edit, and then hand it to Dr. Nemeh on that very special day.

I erupted in tears. They were not due to my past doubts or the lack of time but rather because I couldn't understand why God chose me to do anything. It wasn't that many years ago that I wasn't living a true Christian life. Despite my feelings of unworthiness, I was overjoyed with gratitude and deeply moved by everything He had just revealed to me.

As I wiped my tears and felt His closeness, I rushed home to begin writing.

Philippians 1:6

being confident of this, that he who began a good work in you will carry it on to completion until the day of Christ Jesus.

twenty-six.

GOD KNEW

In just two days, I wrote twelve chapters. I've never written at such a rapid pace in my life, and I think it's reasonable to assume that most authors can't normally write that fast, either. Something like that doesn't seem naturally possible. I have no doubt that I was receiving Divine Assistance in writing this book. From the start, Emily was confident that it would be written quickly. *Boy, was she ever right!* I thought.

I can't say that it was effortless. Despite all the dreams and signs, I was still plagued with countless doubts. I considered the possibility that maybe it was just all wishful thinking.

Ugh! Why am I so wishy-washy...and doubtful? Completing something I felt the Lord calling me to do was a constant battle. Nothing was ever easy.

God once again intervened to help bring His will to light. Just when I needed it, I received an email from the wife of one of Dr. Nemeh's patients. Her husband was brought to Dr. Nemeh by Divine Grace. Due to her husband's stage IV brain cancer, his physician recommended reading the book *Cured: Strengthen Your Immune System and Heal Your Life* by Jeffrey Rediger. In this book, Dr. Rediger devotes an entire chapter to Dr. Nemeh.

A synopsis from the book states:

> *In Cured, Dr. Rediger digs down to the root causes of illness, showing how to create an environment that sets the stage for healing. He reveals the patterns behind healing and lays out the physical and mental principles associated with recovery: first, we need to physically heal our diet and our immune systems. Next, we need to mentally heal our stress response and our identities.*
>
> *Through rigorous research, Dr. Rediger shows that much of our physical reality is created in our minds. Our perception changes our experience, even to the point of changing our physical bodies—and thus the healing of our identity may be our greatest tool to recovery.*
>
> *Ultimately, miracles only contradict what we know of nature at this point in time. Cured leads the way in explaining the*

science behind these miracles, and provides a first-of-its-kind guidebook to both healing and preventing disease.

Shortly after reading this, the woman and her husband decided to investigate more about Dr. Nemeh for themselves. As a result, they attended one of the monthly Zoom calls and later scheduled an office appointment. During their time in his office, they heard about Emily and me being so transformed by what God did for us that we helped bring others to Ohio and that we composed two books about our experiences as well. Although this couple resided in our state, they were still located many hours away from us.

The wife emailed, wanting to express her gratitude for the two books I wrote. She declared that she had thoroughly devoured the first book because the experiences depicted in it were very similar to what they had just gone through. She mentioned that she was about to start reading the second book. Thanks to this thoughtful woman's timely email, I overcame the crushing uncertainties I was experiencing that day. Before receiving it, I was nearly ready to give up on the idea that I was meant to write this book. Thankfully, God always gives us what we need at the right time.

This same lady testified that her husband is now cancer-free! She mentioned that they were striving to trust and disregard the physicians who were already predicting that the cancer would return.

I replied to her email, thanking her for the timely message and letting her know that they would continue to be in our prayers. I concluded by saying that we walk in faith and put our faith into action by placing our mind over matter.

Later in the evening, my son, Joshua, reached out to me. After a brief conversation, he inquired if I would be home tomorrow so that he could come over and have lunch with me. Right away, I sensed that something was not right.

My son is very spontaneous; if he wanted to have lunch with me, he would normally just drop by and see if it would work. It was strange for him to call or ask in advance.

I asked, "What's wrong? Is something wrong?"

There was a moment of hesitation, followed by a heavy sigh.

He stated that his only desire was to come over and talk. I let him know that he was welcome at any time and that I would love for him to come over. As our conversation progressed, he told me he hadn't felt well for some time. Joshua assured me that it wasn't serious, just that he was experiencing low energy, regardless of any changes he made or how long he slept. He also mentioned that he was struggling to gain or maintain his weight.

His weight had been a cause for concern among members of our family. We all took note and shared our worries with each other, and also conveyed them to him as well. Whenever someone asked about his eating habits, Joshua would quickly assure us that he was eating plenty. He'd often say, if anything, he was eating more than most people.

Joshua, who is six-foot tall, further informed me that he was down to one hundred sixty-five pounds. When I heard this, my body immediately tensed up. I had a genuine concern that something was not right. Suddenly, like a flash of light, I had a reminder of that appointment in October come to mind.

I had only recently let him know about my own health scare and the appointment I booked with Dr. Nemeh because of it. I told him the entire situation, including the strange throat pain and how Dr. Nemeh prayed it away due to it being from an old neck injury.

When I told him about those incidents, I explained that I felt confident the issue had been resolved. I conveyed that I was uncertain if I should cancel or wait to see if God had someone in mind to bring there. "We will let God show us who it is for," I told him.

Shortly thereafter, I gained insight into the purpose of the appointment and the intended recipient. While he was talking to me on the phone about coming over for lunch and his troubles with energy and weight, I knew that then was the time to say something about it.

I began by asking, "You are aware of my appointment with Dr. Nemeh in October?"

Josh replied, "Yeah. Why?"

"Well, I have been informed twice now that it is actually for you!"

"You have?!" Joshua asked, sounding completely blindsided.

"That's weird. You didn't seem to know this just a few days ago," Joshua recounted.

"I know," I continued. "Shortly after I told you about it, I had another dream."

As much as I wanted to tell him the entire dream, I knew I had to wait to explain the part about the third book. I would have to tell him about that aspect later and in person.

"I won't bother telling you the whole dream right now, but it involved Dr. Nemeh. In it, he said to me that he would see me soon and then left. I was wondering what that meant, and the date of October 27th came to me."

"After that, I was made aware that I was healed and no longer needed it. As I continued sleeping, I asked who it was for, and just as I posed the question, your face came to me, and I woke up."

A period of awkward silence followed. Josh then asked, "You were asking questions while you were sleeping? Or when you woke up?"

"In my sleep," I answered.

"Huh?! You can do that?"

After sharing my dream with Joshua, we began discussing the distinctions between Heavenly dreams and ordinary ones. Eventually, we returned to the issue of the appointment being for him instead of me.

"You said you have been shown twice? That is only once," Joshua quickly observed.

"Yes, the one I just mentioned was the last time. There was another one, one year ago, almost to the day."

"Do you remember that incredible dream I had last year when God showed me how to approach you about the healing service with Graeson?"

"And that God showed me the entire conversation in advance? Even details about what to ask you and when to go to your house? And He told me that the healing would last forever?"

With a hint of anticipation in his voice, Josh replied, "Uh-huh-h!"

"Well, near the end of that same dream, I also saw that Emily and I would be taking you to see Dr. Nemeh several months down the road."

I paused for a second, hoping he would understand the significance of what I had just said, given the detailed and true nature of that dream.

"When I first had that dream last year, I recorded every aspect of it in my journal so I wouldn't forget one single detail. However, when I documented the part about us taking you to Ohio, and then later shared this final piece of the dream with Emily, I was very skeptical about its significance. Despite knowing that this part of the dream would be for some time in the future, I just thought there was a miscommunication at the end, even though the rest of it was miraculous in every way.

Joshua let out an audible gasp. From what I could tell, he seemed to be as surprised as I was originally.

I reiterated, "Joshua, I understand that it may be hard to believe at first, but I am absolutely positive that this appointment is intended for you. As I stated earlier, I have been shown twice now, but I know I cannot strongarm you into going. You have to want to go."

Once again, there was silence.

"Josh?" I called, wondering if he was still on the line and heard everything or if I lost him and would have to repeat everything again. I pulled my phone away from my ear to double-check that we hadn't been disconnected.

Josh rejoined the conversation by asking, "When is it again? October what?"

Right then, I knew that he would come. Once again, I was impressed by his openness to trusting what I had shared with him.

"The 27th. October 27th," I said faintly, overcome with emotion.

"Okay, Mom, I will go," he vowed.

Jeremiah 29:11-14

For I know the plans I have for you," declares the Lord, "plans to prosper you and not to harm you, plans to give you hope and a future. Then you will call on Me and come and pray to Me, and I will listen to you. You will seek Me and find Me when you seek Me with all your heart. I will be found by you," declares the Lord.

twenty-seven.

GOD IS WITH US

Joshua had previously visited Dr. Nemeh's office in early January of 2020. During that time, he encountered some medical issues that were particularly worrisome and frightening. The week prior to his appointment with Dr. Nemeh, Josh had gone to the emergency room due to intense pressure and pain occurring in his chest.

When I got there, the agony was written all over his face, while occasionally moaning due to the extreme pain he was experiencing. The medical professionals were frantically trying to evaluate what was happening to him. At first sight, the physicians wondered if he was having a heart attack or, worse, an aortic dissection. As precious minutes went by, we were relieved to learn that, thankfully, neither of those guesses were accurate.

During their examination that night, the doctors discovered several nodules on his lungs. We had to wait a few more days before the remaining blood tests were finished. We were alarmed by what they said. In comprehending the severity of the situation, I reached out to Kathy Nemeh for prayers and guidance. After I relayed the blood test results to Kathy, she advised Joshua to come in for an appointment with Dr. Nemeh as soon as possible.

Kathy and Shannon collaborated at the office to arrange an emergency appointment for Joshua only a few days later. Even though Josh's situation was alarming, sadly he didn't have a real desire to go when I passed this information on to him. Being that Josh's diagnosis was not favorable at the time, and his prognosis was less than desirable, his future would already demand numerous medical appointments with one of our local, top-notch pulmonologists. The doctors here were convinced that he had a serious case of histoplasmosis. According to medical data, something this serious could result in a mortality rate of up to 50 percent.

My husband Randy had to get involved and pull the "dad card." He essentially left Joshua with no choice in the matter, instructing him to go see Dr. Nemeh. Randy is a man of few words. Because of this, the kids are very much aware that he tends to be quite serious when he speaks up about something. Joshua heard his father's words and understood that he needed to take this more seriously than he had previously.

On Friday, January 10th, 2020, Emily and I whisked Joshua to Ohio. The circumstances were not ideal, as he felt terrible, was in tremendous pain, and didn't want to go from the beginning. In short, my son was irritable.

During our journey to Ohio, Joshua had something unusual happen. The same phenomenon has been experienced by many others while traveling to their doctor appointment with Dr. Nemeh. Shortly after we started driving, he experienced a significant improvement, and most of his pain had disappeared. Despite being aware of the implications surrounding his likely diagnosis, he felt so great that he thought we should cancel the appointment.

Josh even made a comment wondering if maybe the hospital made a mistake in his diagnosis since he was starting to feel so much better. It seemed to me that he was not thinking logically whatsoever. I attempted to convey to him that what he was going through was something we had seen happening to many others. It's as if God intervenes and offers His grace, assisting people during their journey so they can get to their appointments. Thankfully, I was the one driving and informed him that I had no intention of postponing or canceling his office visit with Dr. Nemeh, regardless of how good he felt.

Kathy texted us while we were traveling and said she could meet us for supper before Josh's appointment. Emily and I were thrilled. Although Josh didn't seem as enthusiastic, he was thankful for the kind gesture and willing to go for a quick bite to eat. Before dinner, the three of us quickly checked into the hotel. Unfortunately, when we dropped off our luggage and were on our way to the restaurant to meet Kathy, Joshua's symptoms started returning in full force. He was experiencing severe pain once again, and it was understandable that his no-nonsense mood resumed along with it.

We met Kathy at Joe's Deli, one of Kathy's favorite local establishments. Emily and I quickly greeted her with a warm hug, '*hello,*' when she approached our table. Josh had no option but to keep his arm held tightly against his chest to help with his breathing and alleviate the pain. When Kathy said hello to him, he could barely muster a quick grin.

She inquired how he was feeling. I knew that she was already aware that he wasn't great. Although she has many spiritual insights like her husband, the Holy Spirit was not required to recognize that Joshua was feeling rather poorly in this instance. Just by looking at him, it was apparent that he wasn't himself. He was as pale as a ghost, extremely thin, exhausted, and clearly in agony.

Our dinner was pleasant, except for my son's occasional moodiness. No one was blaming him for that. We were all mindful of his pain and observed that he was struggling just to concentrate on his meal. I knew by then he was wishing he had stayed behind at the hotel.

Later on in the evening, Joshua, Emily, and I proceeded to Dr. Nemeh's office for the scheduled appointment. Dr. Nemeh invited us in the room and said he would be right back. Emily and I went into the treatment room with Joshua, waiting and praying that everything would turn out okay. Meanwhile, I had been dealing with a bad migraine all day, so truthfully, sometimes it was a struggle for me to stay focused. I was sure that the migraine came on due to the tensions surrounding our situation. Regardless of how bad it got, I knew that I had to push through and be there for my son.

During Dr. Nemeh's treatment, Emily and I both sensed that Josh was experiencing difficulties. From time to time, he appeared to be fascinated by watching Dr. Nemeh and observing his surroundings. But then, like a switch, he would suddenly change his demeanor and appear icy and uninterested. I knew we were witnessing the spiritual battle that was going on in Joshua's head play out right before our very eyes. Because of this, I started to feel somewhat anxious about what might or might not happen.

By the end of the appointment, it appeared that Joshua was becoming increasingly frustrated with himself. Around this time, I felt a sudden surge of heat on the top of my head. Since it was January and it was quite cold out, I initially assumed that I had been feeling the warmth from the furnace turning on. I didn't give much thought to it, but the heat on my head was becoming more intense until it was almost unbearable. It was literally causing my entire head to become uncomfortably hot. I glanced up to see if I was beneath a vent. I was not.

I was completely puzzled by this. Although it only lasted a short while, it was several minutes of INTENSE heat. It took a lot of effort for me to resist the urge to leave my chair. I tried my best to remain still to ensure that Dr. Nemeh's work with Josh wasn't disturbed. During the flash of hotness, Doctor was facing my son with his back towards me. Josh's appointment concluded soon after the heat subsided, and I began to cool down to my normal temperature again.

During his appointment, several remarks were made. Dr. Nemeh made it clear that being cautious while working around fumes was crucial. Days later, Josh's pulmonologist brought up the same issue, suggesting that fume exposure may have been the root cause of his lung issues from the very beginning.

Joshua said he felt no real difference in how he felt as we returned to the hotel that night. All he knew was that he was completely drained. During the night in our hotel room, I awoke and observed that there was a glow covering his entire body. After wiping my eyes, I looked again. *Yep. God is healing him,* I thought to myself and turned over and went back to sleep. I shared with him and Emily about what I saw the next morning.

Emily gave a big smile and asked, "Really?"

Josh, on the other hand, just looked down and didn't say a word. It was evident that he was skeptical about my comments and observations.

Oh well, I pondered to myself. *I know what I saw.*

During breakfast, I recounted how my head suddenly felt hot during the appointment. "It was so strange," I said.

"I even looked up for a vent, but there was nothing. It was quite intense. I almost had to jump out of my seat and move, but I forced myself to stay put so I would not bother Doctor working on you, Josh."

Josh was observing me as I spoke, but as soon as I finished, he quickly glanced back at the ground.

Oh boy, he must really think I am crazy.... Oh well.

I was still uncertain as to what it was, why it happened, or if it had any significance. I just simply chalked it up as a strange incident that happened during Josh's appointment.

Joshua began to improve gradually after we returned home and before his subsequent X-ray and specialist appointments. Several days went by and then Josh dropped by to apologize for his poor behavior during our trip to Ohio. I think he may have felt a sense of guilt when he looked back at how that all came together.

It was evident that he was experiencing less pain and behaving more nicely, as it is expected for anyone's mood to lighten up when their pain decreases.

After the apology, Josh mentioned that he had something else to add.

"Oh yeah, what is that?" I inquired with an amused smile.

"Do you remember the heat you felt on your head during my appointment?"

"Yeah, I remember."

"Well, I had such a hard time staying in the right frame of mind during my appointment. For some reason, I just couldn't keep my mind focused on anything positive. So, well, uh, I finally gave up trying and started redirecting my thoughts on you."

I couldn't figure out what he was talking about and gave him a confused look. Joshua shifted his position, appearing uncomfortable, and then he began gazing down at the floor once more.

"Well, then..." he took a breath, "I asked God to take away your migraine."

I am pretty sure that by this point, my mouth dropped open. I had never put it together that my migraine even left! I was entirely focused on my son.

Josh's eyes were now raised and fixed on me. Both of us stared at each other with tears in our eyes. When Josh heard me give the account of the heat on my head the following morning, he knew that God was definitely present in that room with us. After returning home, Josh slowly began to piece together what had transpired during his appointment. He talked about noticing other minor things that happened, too. I don't believe it's appropriate to label anything he experienced as small. Every miracle is significant, no matter how big or small they may seem.

Joshua experienced a massive shift in his health and outlook over the days ahead. He stopped smoking and was putting his daily life in God's hands. He began to spread the word and even offered to pay for several others to visit Dr. Nemeh. Little by little, his energy returned gradually while the pain continued to disappear until it was completely gone.

I recently reviewed some emails that I sent out *before* that appointment with Dr. Nemeh. Two of them stood out to me.

One of them I wrote to Kathy Nemeh on Friday, January 3rd:

> *I dropped off groceries to Josh (lots of fruit, veggies, eggs, green tea, smoothies, etc.) I told him your words that he "must"*

quit smoking and that you guys would pray for him. I also shared that his condition is probably self-induced and that Emily and I personally think this illness is for a purpose ...to help him along with his faith and to help propel him into where he needs to be....to shake him up a little, so to speak.

On that same day, I also sent a message to my friend Mary Lou Milling, stating:

We have a pretty serious medical issue going on with Josh right now. We were at the ER last night and didn't get home till the middle of the night. I am confident that it will be used for good, and I know it is to help propel Josh into the bigger role God has for him....but right now, it is to shake him up a bit, I think. (I pray that's all).

It was unfortunate that Josh's new way of life didn't last as long as I had hoped. He soon returned to his old habits and routines, putting his time with Dr. Nemeh in 2020 in the past. From that day until now, he had been relatively physically healthy.

Psalm 4:1
Answer me when I call to you,
my righteous God.
Give me relief from my distress;
have mercy on me and hear my prayer.

twenty-eight.

ONCE IN A BLUE MOON

Joshua and I were still on the phone discussing the upcoming appointment that was set for October 27th, 2023, with Dr. Nemeh. After knowing that God had chosen Joshua for the appointed date, my thoughts turned to his health once more. I pondered if he remembered all the things he had gone through in the past. I was aware of the swiftness with which people forget their previous illnesses once they have been healed.

I had to stop thinking about it. Worrying was not going to help in any way. So, I called our dog, Bentley, to take a quick walk while

Joshua remained on the phone talking with me. Randy and Emily took a glance at me, smiled briefly, and acknowledged that I was leaving before they continued with their previous activities. Although they were aware that I was speaking with Josh, they did not grasp that the topic was related to Josh's recent health concerns.

Our conversation continued touching on various topics. I realized it was becoming dark quickly, so I called Bentley to turn around and head back to the house. The last thing I wanted was to encounter a raccoon or another nocturnal animal. After turning around, I proceeded to head east for a moment before I came to an abrupt stop. What I saw had me completely captivated! "Holy cow!" I exclaimed.

"What, Mom?"

"The moon! The moon is rising, and I think it's the biggest moon I have ever seen in my life!"

"Can you see it?" I asked him.

It was the night of the rare "blue supermoon." This unexpected view led us to explore an entirely different topic that only God could orchestrate once again.

I whispered softly, "Signs and wonders."

"What does that mean?"

"In the last days, there will be signs and wonders."

Joshua repeated, thinking I said something entirely different, "Sci..ence? Science and wonders?"

"No, there will be signs and wonders in the last days. S I G N S," I repeated.

"You think the moon being big is a sign?"

" – Don't you think we have been in the last days, like forever?" Josh snuck in before I could answer.

"Have you not heard Dr. Nemeh's talk on the *Blind Faith Live* podcasts about the time to come?" I asked.

Pause. A barely audible "No" came across the line.

"What?!" After all the times I have stressed that you should listen to them…you haven't?"

"And what about the YouTube videos I have sent …you haven't watched those either?"

Once more, a quiet, almost identical, "No."

I asked question after question, "What about 'this' link I sent? What about 'this' video?"

One after the other, he admitted he hadn't looked into anything I sent.

He cut off the frustrated sounds I was making by inquiring, "But, how do you know we are really in the last days, Mom?"

"Because when Jesus was born, it set the clock in motion for when He would come again. It is Biblical fact that He will return."

I continued, "It also says that lawlessness will abound, evil will increase, knowledge shall increase, but there will be a lack of wisdom."

"We are witnessing the formation of a one-world government, a one-world religion, and a one-world currency right before our eyes. These are prophecies that come straight out of the Bible. They are used to indicate if we see these things taking place, that we should pick up our heads. We would no longer be in the "season" of the end, but rather we would be in the (last) days.

"In reading and understanding Scripture, Jesus said He would come for His church after Israel becomes a nation again for the second time. The generation that witnessed Israel doing so will also be witness to Christ's return.

"Israel became a nation for the second time in 1948. It is what Bible scholars call the "super sign," the definitive sign that we are truly in what the Bible calls the "last days" before the return of Christ.

"A generation in that particular context is commonly understood by many Bible scholars to represent a period of up to seventy or eighty years. It is now 2023.

"So, we are aware that the church is nearing the point of being caught up with Christ."

Josh questioned, "Well, I don't know about that. We haven't found any indications to suggest that anyone could be the antichrist."

"I have heard it said that is because he cannot be revealed until we are taken out of here. The Holy Spirit in us, in His Body of Believers, keeps the antichrist from being able to show himself. Once we are gone, the tribulation can start at any time."

Josh knew the rest of the story, finishing it for me, "Yes, the tribulation. In the first three and half years, the antichrist will seem like a good guy. He will be a peacemaker. He will make everything seem great. He will rebuild the third temple in Jerusalem.

"Then he will declare himself as God and make people take the mark."

"Yes!" I said.

I added, "Those living here during that terrible time will not want to take that mark. According to Scripture, 'those who do, will never be able to enter the Kingdom of God.'"

Josh was reflecting on everything and inquired, "But how do you know we won't be here for the first three and a half years? I have heard some Bible teachers say that we will be here for the beginning of God's wrath."

I answered, "Well, I don't know anything for certain, but from what I understand, God's wrath is not for God's people."

"Plus, again, from my understanding, the antichrist cannot come into power until we are gone."

"From what Scripture says and what I understand, the church IS the Restrainer. Specifically, the Holy Spirit in the Body of Christ is the Restrainer. The Holy Spirit is keeping evil at bay. Believe me, I think it could be a lot worse than it is right now."

After our bantering back and forth, Josh let out a whispered, "Wow!"

My thoughts were also, '*Wow!*'

I believe that the Holy Spirit was speaking through me during our entire conversation because, in most cases, I couldn't have revealed everything I did without the Holy Spirit's guidance. Normally, I would have had to refer to the Bible or locate a quote, but I didn't need to that night.

I have been listening to and learning from Dr. Nemeh for a while now and have discovered others like him who are spreading awareness and educating people about the times we are currently living in by referencing Biblical prophecies. Despite the state of the world and all that's to come, they all affirm that we have no reason to be sad or worried as we anticipate "The Blessed Hope" of our Lord's return.

I continued with Joshua, "It seems that all the boxes have been checked. All the prophecies for that BIG event have been fulfilled or are still currently being fulfilled. He could literally come at any moment."

It was apparent that what I said had made an impression, "What are the names of the videos you mentioned before?" He asked.

I let him know and then told him I had so many other things I needed to say to him, but if I did, we would be on the phone all night.

Josh laughed but then quickly asked, "Wait!...What?! What other things?"

"I will talk with you tomorrow when you come by for lunch. What time works for you? I am very flexible," I said, quivering due to the chill of the evening air and the excitement from our conversation filling my body.

"How about noon?" Josh asked. "Does that work for you?"

"It sure does. I will make you a healthy lunch. Grilled steak with a Greek salad. See you tomorrow, my son. I love you!"

"I love you, too, Mom."

I was left standing outside in total silence, captivated by what just took place. As I gazed eastward to the heavens, I observed the brilliant moon slowly and silently drifting into the night sky. I could hardly believe how our conversation had gone. Seeing the rising of that rare and enormous blue moon was significant in helping me convey the urgency of the times we now live to my son.

I first typed this on Tuesday, September 5, 2023. It was fitting that the first reading for the Daily Catholic Mass on that day was the following:

1 Thes 5:1-6, 9-11

Concerning times and seasons, brothers and sisters,

you have no need for anything to be written to you.

For you yourselves know very well

that the day of the Lord will come like a thief at night.

When people are saying, "Peace and security,"

then sudden disaster comes upon them,

like labor pains upon a pregnant woman,

and they will not escape.

But you, brothers and sisters, are not in darkness,

for that day to overtake you like a thief.

For all of you are children of the light

and children of the day.

We are not of the night or of darkness.

Therefore, let us not sleep as the rest do,

but let us stay alert and sober.

For God did not destine us for wrath,

but to gain salvation through our Lord Jesus Christ,

who died for us, so that whether we are awake or asleep

we may live together with him.

Therefore, encourage one another and build one another up,

as indeed you do.

Luke 21:20-33

"When you see Jerusalem being surrounded by armies, you will know that its desolation is near. Then let those who are in Judea flee to the mountains, let those in the city get out, and let those in the country not enter the city. For this is the time of punishment in fulfillment of all that has been written. How dreadful it will be in those days for pregnant women and nursing mothers! There will be great distress in the land and wrath against this people. They will fall by the sword and will be taken as prisoners to all the nations. Jerusalem will be trampled on by the Gentiles until the times of the Gentiles are fulfilled.

"There will be signs in the sun, moon and stars. On the earth, nations will be in anguish and perplexity at the roaring and tossing of the sea. People will faint from terror, apprehensive of what is coming on the world, for the heavenly bodies will be shaken. At that time they will see the Son of Man coming in a cloud with power and great glory. When these things begin to take place, stand up and lift up your heads, because your redemption is drawing near."

He told them this parable: "Look at the fig tree and all the trees. When they sprout leaves, you can see for yourselves and know that summer is near. Even so, when you see these things happening, you know that the kingdom of God is near.

"Truly I tell you, this generation will certainly not pass away until all these things have happened. Heaven and earth will pass away, but my words will never pass away.

twenty-nine.

WHO DO YOU SAY HE IS?

On the very next day, Josh came by for lunch. I noted his attire was not what I would expect to see on the last day of August. While sporting sunglasses on his head as he entered the door, he was also wearing several long-sleeved shirts and work jeans. He came into the kitchen while still wearing his work boots and greeted me with a hug.

Despite the calendar still indicating that we were in the month of August, the day was sunny and crisp, with a hint of fall in the air. We opted to eat outside on the deck to take advantage of the cooler weather we were experiencing.

I had prepared two rather large ribeye steaks and a sizeable salad to share. We each divided one steak in half and took a portion of the salad. Josh finished his food quickly and was on his way to grab seconds. My son was telling the truth about how much food he could eat. Even so, I noticed his slim physique when he went inside to get more.

In the beginning, we had engaged in some small talk, but Josh was soon interested in knowing more about "the many other things" that I previously referred to on the phone. I reminded him that he was the one that first proposed having lunch together primarily because he needed to talk with me about something. Our conversation had become so ridiculous that by then, we were both laughing.

We began to talk about his weight and lack of energy. I expressed that a flame of fear sparked inside me when he mentioned that both of those issues were occurring simultaneously. I stated the combination of those two symptoms happening at the same time is usually never a good thing.

It became evident that he hadn't put that together until then. Initially, I was embarrassed for causing him more anxiety by saying that, but then I realized that he may have needed to hear it. *Perhaps he needed to comprehend the seriousness of the situation,* I thought.

I didn't want to think that way, but I also didn't want to brush everything under the rug and assume he was perfectly fine either.

Regardless of the situation, I have come to realize that God had a plan for him and his situation for more than a year now. God knew ahead of time what was going to happen.

We spoke again about that dream I had and when I was informed that the appointment was meant for him.

I then asked, "Joshua, do you remember all that Jesus has done for you?"

He quietly replied, "Yes." Although, I don't think he was considering the incident with his lungs in 2020. It's likely that he was only thinking about when Graeson prayed for him last year.

There was a brief silence. My serious expression left him looking puzzled and caused a small line to form on his forehead. I squinted at Josh, trying to pray about how to proceed, while he remained silent.

At once, I had the knowledge of how to proceed. My plan was to ask the same question that Kathy Nemeh did in her most recent monthly *Path to Faith* Newsletter.

I continued, questioning Josh, "Okay, and who do you say HE is?"

I sat there staring and waiting for an answer.

Josh looked more confused than ever. I repeated, "Who do you say HE is?"

Josh studied my face. Then I could see the lightbulb moment had come. He became more aware of what I was implying through my questions.

He still seemed uncertain about where this was going and responded slowly and hesitantly with one word, "Jesus."

I spoke again, "He saved you that special day last year. Yes?"

"Who is HE to you? Is HE your Lord? Do you live for HIM? Do you acknowledge all that HE has done for you?"

Following my inquiry, we experienced another uncomfortable moment between us.

I noticed that I had caught him off guard at first, but now he was contemplating everything I had asked him.

Suddenly, our shade had disappeared. The temperature on the back deck was rising due to the sun's arrival, making it warmer than it was comfortable. We stepped inside, grabbing a barstool to continue talking around our kitchen island.

Then came Josh's turn to ask questions. He was curious about what I meant the night before. What else did I need to talk to him about? He desperately wanted to know.

I began my reply by asking him again if he had started reading my books yet. "Or have you started listening to them with the link I provided you?"

"There was a good reason I asked those questions the other day," I stated matter of factly.

“What?! Oh no! What does that mean?” he asked with a look of apprehension.

"Do you recall when I mentioned that I would be writing book number three the other day?"

Josh nodded.

I fidgeted, chuckled nervously, and prayed for guidance on how to handle the matter, saying, "Welllll..."

“Um...well, Josh...your story is in it. You know the part where Graeson prayed for you?” I blurted.

Josh's eyes were filled with a mixture of shock and confusion. I certainly startled him with my comment.

“What? I never even told you everything about my story…or about what happened during my prayer. How could you write my story if you don’t even know the whole thing?” He wondered.

“I know that Josh. This book will be written solely from my perspective."

Josh exuded a slight sense of relief upon hearing those words.

I pointed out, "It is not necessary for me to know the details that you haven’t shared with me. Those are personal and are for you. But…the story as it is, I have to write it solely from my perspective.” I kept praying intensely for the Holy Spirit to guide my words.

“I don’t know how to tell you this, so I will just say it. I have heard others say things like, 'I heard from God the Father. Or the

Holy Spirit...' Those statements were always so strange to me. I never understood it until it happened to me."

Josh was leaning in, looking to prepare himself for what I would say next.

"Last September, I had a dream where God the Father spoke to me about you. He instructed me to write about the healing He gave you. I understood that when I eventually wrote about it, I was supposed to include the details about Graeson. I WAS OVERWHELMED WITH MANY THOUGHTS when I woke up that next day.

"Josh, first, I had a dream where God, the FATHER, had spoken to me. The FATHER, Josh!" I exclaimed.

"I mean, yeah, there is the Trinity, God the Father, the Son, and the Holy Spirit. But when I think about God the Father as a separate entity, that is pretty intimidating for some reason."

That statement gave Josh a good laugh.

I continued, "But back then, I just didn't understand why...or how...I should write a book that included Graeson. I was very confused. I was unsure if it meant that I needed to write the entire book featuring Graeson and somehow included your miracle story or how to go about it."

"I just could not for the life of me comprehend the essence of it. I was constantly thinking, trying to grasp how this would all come together."

Josh was nodding, following along.

"Okay, and now, almost a year to the day later, I had the dream where I was shown the appointment in October was meant for you. I know it is for you because your face was illuminated right before me, just as you sit here with me right now. It was so real.

"I haven't told you everything yet. I presented Dr. Nemeh with a stack of three books just prior to being shown the October date and having your face come to me.

"I knew that the two books on the bottom were the ones I had already written, while the top one was my third book. A book I hadn't even started writing yet. But there it was, sitting right on top, completely finished, and I was giving it to Dr. Nemeh. I became aware that every book contained accounts of miracles that God had carried out, with the majority of them coming from those we had brought to Dr. Nemeh.

"Josh, the most important aspect was that I knew I would have to start writing it as soon as possible. I would have it completely finished and hand it to him during your October appointment! I also knew *for absolute certain* that your story would be included in this book."

"At first, I thought, 'this is impossible!' BUT then I remembered all I have witnessed in the past few years, and I know that anything really is possible *with God*!

"Sooo...after that I began writing the very next morning, and in the past three and a half days, I have written over fourteen chapters."

Josh's eyes widened as he stared at me with a look of amazement and disbelief.

"I know, right!? It almost seems too good to be true."

"When I first started writing, I was remembering the recent times that I had lost my way. Not once, but multiple times, I got lost. Do you remember all of this, Josh? When I mentioned that my knots and pain were returning? How terrified I was thinking that the lupus had returned?"

Josh was nodding, acknowledging that he had heard this before, paying close attention to my every word. His eyes were glued on me while he strained to follow where I was headed with all of this.

"I let you know that I had experienced intense suffering for many weeks but finally realized that my healing was still intact. The only thing I needed to do was return to what God had healed me to do and believe that I was healed. To remember that my life was now dedicated to helping others, and not to waste it doing meaningless activities. My days are meant to count for something.

"I was able to find my way back to Him after conducting hours of research. I was praying again and following what He had placed on my heart. But this didn't just happen the one time. It occurred multiple times. I don't know why, but I kept forgetting the lessons I had learned. I would have to retrain myself on everything again.

"Me, Josh... your mom, who has seen so many miracles...and been taught so many lessons! Even though I am aware that Jesus saved me in 2019, I still was able to become so distracted when something caught me off guard, which would lead me to lose sight of what was most important in life. And whenever it happened, I would get lost in the chaos."

I stopped. I took a deep breath and concluded, "Joshua, I believe this is also a part of what's happening with you. On that day, when Graeson prayed with you, Jesus saved you, just like He did with me years earlier. He removed your heart of stone and gave you His. My belief is He carried out this action with the hopeful expectation that you would abide by His plans for your life."

Even though we were still sitting in the kitchen, Josh suddenly grabbed his sunglasses. Putting them on and covering his eyes, he tried to hide his emotions that had started to stir.

I carried on, "This book that I am working on, Joshua... It is meant to share that healing story that He did for you and the ones He has done for me repeatedly."

"Initially, I was quite unsure how I was supposed to move forward when I dreamed of God the Father asking me to write about your healing. But now that I've started the process, everything is beginning to make sense. I was trying to figure out how to incorporate both Graeson and Dr. Nemeh. But then, while writing these stories, it became clear to me that there was nothing to figure out. God was the connection; He was the link. It was God who was the primary factor, not anyone else.

"Although these men are fulfilling their vocations and allowing God to work in their lives, the miracles are solely attributed to the Lord. He is the One who is healing everyone. He is the One who loves us so much that He desires to heal us. Furthermore, He is working tirelessly all around us, trying to shake people awake to the realities of the times we live in right now. That's what this book was to be about.

"The purpose of this book is to reveal many things, but it basically boils down to the unique times we're currently living in. He healed you and me, saving us along the way so that we can, in turn, reach out and help others understand the closeness of that special day. His nearness is quickly approaching."

I could see the tears coming into view, running down Josh's cheeks as I spoke.

"Without God's hand in all of it, I couldn't write so many chapters in such a short time, nor would I be able to have such amazing and prophetic dreams. You have the option to say that you don't want to be in the book, but honestly, I will still have to write about it. If you don't want to be mentioned, I can alter your name and relationship to me to conceal your identity. All I know is that

I must do it, and after months of confusion, He finally revealed the way to move forward. I must listen, knowing that there is likely a greater purpose for it than even I can imagine."

For a considerable amount of time, Josh bowed his head. He seemed to be not only contemplating what to do but also praying. Removing his sunglasses, he lifted his head, looked me straight in the eye, and said, "I give you permission to write about my story."

"Josh, I am aware that some of the stories may be sensitive. However, I am confident that whatever the Holy Spirit inspires me to write will have spiritual insights that will be beneficial to all those who read it."

After that, I spoke about the significant changes that *The Blessed Reason Trip* had gone through.

"We have just established ourselves as a nonprofit. The focus of our website now is to educate people on the various ways they can receive God's healing. The purpose has changed to include more than just directing people to Dr. Nemeh. The goal is to show how God is rapidly moving to heal and inform people from all over about the upcoming Biblical event. We are confident that is why the number of miracles is growing, happening in such great numbers.

"Christians need to wake up from their lukewarmness. It's simple: we either stand for Christ one hundred percent or we don't."

Romans 13:11

And do this, understanding the present time: The hour has already come for you to wake up from your slumber, because our salvation is nearer now than when we first believed.

thirty.

THE REDEMPTIVE ACT

These past four years have been such a blessing for Emily and me as we have witnessed numerous people being touched and restored. Jesus has been observed addressing everything, from the most minor concerns to the most significant ones that lead to a complete spiritual transformation. In my previous books, I have given a detailed description of some of those amazing life-changing stories.

When God first inspired me to write this book, He indicated that the title should be *The Power of God Yesterday*. It was unclear to me then why the title contained the word 'yesterday' after all the other topics I had already covered. Through God's guidance, I understood I needed to add something I had neglected to include in the previous two books. It was something I learned about in the past, but without explaining this missing concept now, the mystery surrounding the miracles would not be complete. It is a significant factor that has influenced the Christian's past, present, and future. The time had finally come for me to write about it.

The heart of everything God is doing to reveal Himself to so many people around the world revolves around this same premise. I was initially introduced to it by Dr. Nemeh in 2011 when we attended our very first healing service near Chicago to address a worrisome growth on Emily's ribcage. Even though Dr. Nemeh's message was important, my thoughts were preoccupied with my daughter's well-being. I lost sight of his words because of the distraction of seeing the Spirit of God heal people for the first time and being in an unfamiliar environment. That day, I was not in the proper mindset to focus on such profound concepts.

Despite my inability to pay close attention, Dr. Nemeh's words still made an impression on me. I had a general idea of the subject and the implications he made during his short speech before he began to pray individually with everyone in attendance. Surprisingly, I remembered that it had something to do with being a follower of Christ and the greater impact we make in the world.

Dr. Nemeh touched on it again in his Ohio treatment room in 2019. I still didn't fully understand the central part of his message. Thankfully, we ended our stay on that trip by attending another one of Dr. Nemeh's healing services held at a nearby hotel. Dr. Nemeh spoke to the room before the prayers started, just as he did in 2011. I was fortunate enough to hear the message again because that day, it finally penetrated my heart.

Dr. Nemeh has consistently stressed one topic from the first time I heard him speak in 2011 until now. What is happening spiritually in today's world is directly connected to this theory that he talks about. It is about the Redemption process that begins with Christ and ends once the number of servants of God has been fulfilled.

Dr. Nemeh commonly begins his events by talking about the disruptive event that altered the perfect order of God's creation. Specifically, when one-third of all angels fell, which was long before Adam and Eve came into being.

In Revelation 12:4, John writes:

"[Satan's] tail swept a third of the stars out of the sky and flung them to the earth.

In this Scripture passage, stars symbolize angels, indicating that Satan and his angels were expelled from Heaven. We are given insight into the major battle that took place in Heaven. One that the devil and his angels lost when they were cast down to earth.

In Dr. Nemeh's message, it is revealed that we, as followers of Christ, are involved in a Redemptive Act to help remedy this wrong that took place. Dr. Nemeh further states that every time a believer surrenders their life entirely to Christ, that person is matching one of those fallen ones. Thereby also progressively blocking their influence on the body of Christ upon this earth. Pulling out a Bible was all it took for me to clearly see that what he mentioned was Scriptural.

Revelation 6:11 NASB:

And there was given to each of them a white robe; and they were told that they should rest for a little while longer, until the number of their fellow servants and their brethren who were to be killed even as they had been, should be completed also.

According to Doctor, until those who offer their lives to Christ reaches the number of angels who fell from Heaven for refusing to serve God is reached, the matching will be ongoing. Eventually, this number will be achieved, and the Church, the Body of Christ, specifically those who live for Him, will rise as a whole.

Because of this matching, Dr. Nemeh argues that evil is not as powerful as it used to be despite its constant roar around us. The truth is, it's quite the opposite. Evil recognizes that its time is short due to the neutralizing that has been ongoing for over two thousand years.

Revelation 12:12

"He is filled with fury, because he knows that his time is short."

Evil's weakness is most evident in the aggressiveness we see today. Evil is becoming more desperate, which is why it no longer hides itself the way it used to. It was once considered shameful to do evil things in the past, but nowadays, it is often overlooked and tolerated, sometimes even celebrated.

Dr. Nemeh suggests that the matching of Christians to the fallen evil angels correlates with the upcoming events in the Church. His words captivated me, prompting me to read and analyze Scripture passages. I noticed that Dr. Nemeh's remarks are in line with what is stated in the Bible.

It is Dr. Nemeh's belief that we are very close to this event. He recognizes that the fulfillment of countless Biblical prophecies from thousands of years ago has currently surpassed any other period in history. The many signs that God is giving us is meant to indicate the season we are in and the proximity of this great event.

The signs around us suggest that this event will occur within our lifetime. Before that historic moment, someone will assist in bringing that last soul into the family of God. And when this grand moment occurs, and the very last person repents in this present age, the long-awaited judgment will begin. Dr. Nemeh suggests it could theoretically happen at any time.

Matthew 24:42

"Therefore keep watch, because you do not know on what day your Lord will come.

thirty-one.

THE GREAT EXCHANGE

In writing this final chapter, I am reminded of the way the Lord brought Kathy and Dr. Nemeh into our lives. Our healings were so meaningful that they led us to want to share what was possible through the Nemeh's prayers and God's love with others. So, in May 2019, we took a major leap of faith and put together our first bus trip, taking people to Ohio to witness for themselves what this was all about.

I recall Dr. Nemeh standing at the podium and stressing the importance of our current times to the group. Dr. Nemeh touched on a variety of topics that he was inspired to share with us.

Throughout the entire weekend, and until we returned home, his words continued to move us and were the topic of many discussions within our group.

Dr. Nemeh talked about the matching again, but this time, something else caught my attention. He emphasized the importance of not conforming to this world but rather becoming transformed by renewing our minds in Christ.

Dr. Nemeh's words stayed with me when we returned from our bus trip. To gain a better understanding of what he was referring to, I returned to the Scriptures once more.

> *Romans 12:1-2 NIV*
>
> *A Living Sacrifice*
>
> *Therefore, I urge you, brothers and sisters, in view of God's mercy, to offer your bodies as a living sacrifice, holy and pleasing to God—this is your true and proper worship. Do not conform to the pattern of this world, but be transformed by the renewing of your mind. Then you will be able to test and approve what God's will is—His good, pleasing and perfect will.*

I learned that renewing our mind is a process that requires dying to sin and living to righteousness until our soul becomes perfected in glory. However, conformity to this world is our greatest stumbling block to this renewal.

If we conform to the world, we follow its ways and fall prey to the world's pleasures. They are only an illusion meant to distract us from what truly matters: God and His Kingdom. Jesus tells us to seek first His Kingdom and His Righteousness. Those are the holy things that deserve our attention.

It is all meant to be a journey for us to rid ourselves of our negative attributes, let go of our ego, and humble ourselves before the Lord. We have to live in the world, but we should not be a part of it. Our love for the Lord is the starting point for changing our way of thinking. This love will then culminate into our total surrender. The same surrender that is necessary to be a part of the Redemptive Act.

By understanding our life's journey in Christ, we are allowing our lives to be used as a spiritual act of worship. This is what it means to live a transformed life. This is the act of living for Jesus and offering ourselves as a living sacrifice.

The events happening around us today require us as Christians to make decisions, whether they are right or wrong. The Lord uses this method to move us out of lukewarmness and determine if we are hot or cold. According to what I have heard through Dr. Nemeh, he perceives these events as a means of purifying the church. God is weeding out the weak ones, and even though the strong ones are a minority, they are being strengthened in the process. Those who truly identify with Christ are working together, striving for truth and righteousness in their words and actions. They truly desire to follow Jesus, teach others, and proclaim His Word.

Our goal is to reach the number through our evangelization. Once we have fulfilled our purpose of existence, the Lord will take action. And then, He will completely block the evil mind, allowing the Mercy of God to fall on all nations and those who gave their lives as a sacrifice.

Dr. Nemeh talks about the great blessing of living in this moment. By renewing our minds and taking necessary steps towards spiritual transformation, we are aiding in the establishment of the Kingdom of God. We can do this by exchanging the lies for truth, exchanging the natural way of thinking for God's way of thinking. The choices we make ultimately determine whether or not we fulfill our God-given destiny. Each one of us has a predestined function within the Body of Christ once we fully belong to Him.

When we surrender entirely by offering ourselves and remain still in our love for Him, He will begin to make Himself and His Will known to us. God will show us the way by directing our paths, even though our understanding is limited at the time. The Holy Spirit has a far-reaching outlook on the future ahead of us.

I was made aware of this truth when God showed me a year in advance that Joshua would require another appointment with Dr. Nemeh. Likewise, God often utilizes us in the present moment to ultimately bless and make a difference in the lives of those around us in the future.

For me, one thing seems to stand out as having made the biggest difference in my life, and it perfectly aligns with what Dr. Nemeh speaks about. It is that my spiritual life depends heavily on my mental state. This was made evident when I went through endless doubts, serious life challenges, and losing my way multiple times. I have seen the results of what follows once I shift my focus to seeking God with all my heart, soul, and mind.

The only way to find true meaning and purpose in this life is through Jesus Christ. His love for us is such that He values us enough to call us to do great things for the Kingdom of God while we are here on earth. It helps me understand this life and puts everything in perspective. Furthermore, each of us has been called and equipped by God to share the Gospel and help reach the matching number of fallen angels.

The foundation for living the right way and having the right state of mind for Christians is prayer. I have repeatedly observed that when we call on the Lord's name, He hears us. Anything is possible when we pray according to His will.

Dr. Nemeh is the person who most effectively demonstrates this truth in my life, and his position remains unwavering. The healing of the mind is more important to him than the healing of the body. Although Dr. Nemeh tries to reach people in different ways, it always comes back to this truth.

Many physical healings help to bring about the healing of the mind, which can lead a person to discover how to live with the right intention and recognize the value of their life – which is the *ultimate* healing. This is what helps us to overcome this world. We are the heart of the battle for the establishment of the Kingdom of God. As Christians, we accept both our blessings and sufferings and offer them up to God, showing Him our complete devotion no matter what comes our way. Belonging to Jesus makes us different. It teaches us that everything is a blessing and serves a purpose.

Life's trials can cause our hearts to harden like stone. But the Lord has been working to transform many hearts by replacing hardened ones with a true heart of flesh, just as He did for my son. The numerous healings happening all around us make it easy for people to observe how Jesus is moving at a rapid pace.

By healing and opening hearts, God's mission is to illuminate His love for us and allow us to discover our higher purpose in this life. It was the same when He walked the earth. Many who saw the healings came to believe in Him and then follow Him. That is how the Lord started, and that is the way the church began.

An urgency exists in our times, just as it did back then. The season we are currently experiencing is noticeable to many people, particularly when prophecies are being fulfilled. It is a sign of His nearness. It is time for us to wake up, reorder our lives, make Him our primary focus, and align our hearts back to God. He is providing us with many signs to help us gain this awareness.

As faith-filled Believers, it is time for us to act. Too many Christians are either asleep, distracted, or intoxicated by the world. It's essential to communicate to our loved ones and friends how God is moving today. He is urging us to wake up, be watchful and vigilant, and stop being indifferent about our faith.

Recognizing the value of our lives is essential. This is the path to overcoming evil and this fallen world. This is also the way to achieve the ultimate healing. By understanding our worth, we serve Jesus in the matching, helping to restore the love that was lost and build up the Kingdom of God. It's a matter of one person at a time offering their life onto the Lord and finishing the matching that has been ongoing for thousands of years.

We eagerly await our Lord, not as orphans, but rather as citizens of Heaven. And when the time is ripe, Paul tells us that our Savior "will transform our lowly bodies so that they will be like His glorious body." Philippians 3:20-21

Although we don't know the day or the hour, Jesus and the prophets from the days of old have prophesied thousands of years in advance so that we would know the season. It's important to live as if He's ready to come back, as if His hand is on the door, so to speak. We want to be found watching and ready for His return. We want to hear those words, '*Well done, good and faithful servant.*'

1Peter 1:13-16

Therefore, with minds that are alert and fully sober, set your hope on the grace to be brought to you when Jesus Christ is revealed at His coming.

As obedient children, do not conform to the evil desires you had when you lived in ignorance. But just as He who called you is holy, so be holy in all you do; for it is written: "Be holy, because I am holy."

acknowledgements.

I would like to express my heartfelt gratitude to everyone who has contacted me to share their personal journeys with me over the past few years. I am thankful for the friendships that have developed with many of you and for the connections we've made throughout our journey.

A Special Thank You

Kathy and Dr. Issam Nemeh, I want to express my utmost appreciation for everything you have taught me. Thanks to you, I have developed and strengthened my relationship with Jesus Christ. Your presence here on earth has played a significant role in aiding individuals like myself on our spiritual journey through life. You both play a crucial role in bringing the gospel to life in a way that no one else does. Whenever we have called, texted, emailed, or were praying on our knees, you have always been there for us. I am deeply thankful for your friendship and contribution to our lives.

Appreciation for Friends

I would like to express my gratitude to my friend Graeson Dall. I cannot thank you enough for your unwavering support and willingness to assist our family on multiple occasions. I am delighted to witness how God is using you and your ministry to assist those in need of prayer on a daily basis. You truly are a servant of Christ in every way.

I am grateful to a number of friends and family members who have prayed for me during the challenging times of the past year. Your love and support played a crucial role in me completing the writing of this book. It's not necessary for me to mention names because you already know who you are. Your powerful prayers have been instrumental in lifting me out of the muck and returning me to solid ground on countless occasions. My life wouldn't be complete without each and every one of you, and I am eternally grateful for it.

My Husband and Children

I am deeply grateful to my family. Your love, prayers, and support make it possible for me to write about what God has done for us and those around us. My husband consistently provided me with wise and loving words when I encountered a challenge.

Joshua, my son, was truly gracious in allowing me to include the healing of his heart, which is a deeply personal matter. Your willingness to help others by sharing what God has done for you is incredibly beautiful and inspiring. Thank you! Your unwavering devotion to Him during tough times is something I admire. You have no idea how much this blesses me.

Collette, my oldest daughter, was so receptive in letting me share a portion of her story about how God is beginning to manifest in her life. Not only is it an amazing display of love towards me, but it also benefits many other parents. It illustrates that a parent must never give up on the possibility of their children returning back to God.

At this moment, my son Matthew and his wife Allie are celebrating the arrival of our new addition to the family, their daughter, Stella Joy Blake, who was born on November 5th, 2023. Their presence in our family brings us immense joy. The love they possess within is reflected in how they live their lives. It is all quite beautiful! All three of you are very dear to me.

Forever Indebted

To my youngest daughter, my confidant and spiritual companion. Emily – you and I have been on the best journey of our lives since Dr. and Kathy Nemeh entered our lives four years ago. I cannot express how grateful I am for everything you do for me. You are always willing to help me with anything and everything without fail. I receive encouragement from you every day, regardless of whether I am writing or not. By reading and editing the roughest of drafts, you have been a crucial part of my writing process for each of these books. Likewise, your efforts in designing and creating the cover for each of The Power of God Series books has contributed to making them what they are today. I'm not sure how to express my appreciation for everything you do apart from saying that I love you.

Most grateful to Jesus

My ultimate thank you is to thank my Lord and Savior, Jesus Christ. I place You above all else and understand that being called to do anything for You is far beyond my worth. Despite that, I feel blessed every time You call on me, and it was truly amazing how this book could be written in a rough draft form in such a short period of time. Without the help of the Holy Spirit, it would be impossible to do so. Everyone who reads this should remember that God has the power to make anything happen.

Jesus, I was overwhelmed by Your Loving Presence during the difficult and lonely hours of revision and editing. There were weeks where I didn't leave the house except to attend Mass and worship You. You made sure I knew You were with me every step of the way throughout the rest of the week. Because of it, my life will never be the same again.

-Your grace is enough, Lord.

Corinthians 12:9

But He said to me, "My grace is sufficient for you, for my power is made perfect in weakness."

from my own journal speaking to Jesus dated 2/29/20:

I know what I saw...

I believe what I have learned...

and I love what I have found.

divine mercy chaplet.

How to Pray the Divine Mercy Chaplet:

You can pray the Chaplet at any time, but 3:00 p.m. is known as the "hour of great mercy" in remembrance of Christ's death on the cross at 3:00 p.m. on Good Friday. Similarly, people often pray the Stations of the Cross at this time.

Using regular Rosary beads (or your ten fingers), follow this structure:

Begin with the sign of the cross.

In the name of the Father, and of the Son, and of the Holy Spirit. Amen.

Pray, preparing your heart and mind.

You expired, Jesus, but the source of life gushed forth for souls, and the ocean of mercy opened up for the whole world. O Fount of Life, unfathomable Divine Mercy, envelop the whole world and empty Yourself out upon us.

Pray the prayer of St. Faustina.

On each of the three small beads, pray:

O Blood and Water, which gushed forth from the Heart of Jesus as a fount of mercy for us, I trust in You! (x3)

Pray an Our Father.

Our Father, Who art in heaven, hallowed be Thy name; Thy kingdom come; Thy will be done on earth as it is in heaven. Give us this day our daily bread; and forgive us our trespasses as we forgive those who trespass against us; and lead us not into temptation, but deliver us from evil, Amen.

Pray a Hail Mary.

Hail Mary, full of grace. The Lord is with thee. Blessed art thou amongst women, and blessed is the fruit of thy womb, Jesus. Holy Mary, Mother of God, pray for us sinners, now and at the hour of our death, Amen.

Pray the Apostle's Creed.

I believe in God, the Father almighty, Creator of heaven and earth, and in Jesus Christ, his only Son, our Lord, who was conceived by the Holy Spirit, born of the Virgin Mary, suffered under Pontius Pilate, was crucified, died and was buried; He descended into hell; on the third day He rose again from the dead; He ascended into heaven, and is seated at the right hand of God the Father almighty; from there He will come to judge the living and the dead. I believe in the Holy Spirit, the holy catholic Church, the communion of saints, the forgiveness of sins, the resurrection of the body, and life everlasting. Amen.

First decade

On the first large bead: in the traditional Rosary prayer, we say the Our Father for each large bead. In the Divine Mercy Chaplet, we pray the following:

Eternal Father, I offer you the Body and Blood, Soul and Divinity of Your Dearly Beloved Son, Our Lord, Jesus Christ, in atonement for our sins and those of the whole world.

On the ten small beads:

In a traditional Rosary prayer, we pray the Hail Mary on each small bead. In the Divine Mercy Chaplet, we pray the following:

For the sake of His sorrowful Passion, have mercy on us and on the whole world. (x10)

Repeat this pattern four times. For each decade: begin with the "Eternal Father" prayer, and then pray, "For the sake" ten times.

After five decades, pray for mercy.

Repeat the following prayer three times:

Holy God, Holy Mighty One, Holy Immortal One, have mercy on us and on the whole world. (x3)

Close your time in prayer.

Let us pray: Eternal God, in whom mercy is endless and the treasury of compassion — inexhaustible, look kindly upon us and increase Your mercy in us, that in difficult moments we might not despair nor become despondent, but with great confidence submit ourselves to Your holy will, which is Love.

Conclude with the sign of the cross. In the name of the Father and of the Son and of the Holy Spirit, Amen.

about the author.

Christine M. Blake and her daughter Emily had tremendous healings on all levels in January 2019. These amazing transformations were primarily due to the prayers and faith from Dr. Issam Nemeh. Since that time, Christine and her daughter Emily have dedicated their lives to helping others learn about Dr. Issam and Kathy Nemeh and the ways our Lord is still walking and healing us today.

More information can be found about Christy & Emily by going to their website:
www.theblessedreasontrip.org

To learn more about Dr. Issam Nemeh visit:
www.pathtofaith.com

Made in the USA
Monee, IL
27 January 2024

51744948R10187